"And Then Justin Told Sergio..."

"And Then Justin Told Sergio..."

A Collection of the Greatest True Golf Stories Ever Told

DON WADE
Foreword by Gary Player

Contemporary Books

Chicago New York San Francisco Lisbon London Madrid Mexico City
Milan New Delhi San Juan Seoul Singapore Sydney Toronto

Library of Congress Cataloging-in-Publication Data

Wade, Don.
    "And then Justin told Sergio . . ." : a collection of the greatest
true golf stories ever told / Don Wade ; foreword by Gary Player ;
[illustrations by Paul Szep].
        p.   cm.
    ISBN 0-8092-9470-2 (alk. paper)
    1. Golf—Anecdotes.   I. Title.

GV967.W2695   2002
796.352—dc21   2001047758

Contemporary Books

A Division of The **McGraw·Hill** Companies

1 2 3 4 5 6 7 8 9 0   LBM/LBM   1 0 9 8 7 6 5 4 3 2

ISBN 0-8092-9470-2

This book was set in Clearface
Printed and bound by Lake Book Manufacturing

Illustrations by Paul Szep

McGraw-Hill books are available at special quantity discounts to use as
premiums and sales promotions, or for use in corporate training programs.
For more information, please write to the Director of Special Sales,
Professional Publishing, McGraw-Hill, Two Penn Plaza, New York, NY
10121-2298. Or contact your local bookstore.

This book is printed on acid-free paper.

For Julia, Ben, Darcy, Andy,
and all the Concord Wades

Other Books by Don Wade

"And Then Jack Said to Arnie . . ."
"And Then Arnie Told Chi Chi . . ."
"And Then Chi Chi Told Fuzzy . . ."
"And Then Fuzzy Told Seve . . ."
"And Then Seve Told Freddie . . ."
"And Then Freddie Told Tiger . . ."
"And Then Tiger Told the Shark . . ."
"And Then the Shark Told Justin . . ."
Talking on Tour

CONTENTS

FOREWORD

I was very lucky because when I joined the PGA Tour in 1957, many of the great champions I had read and heard so much about as a boy growing up were still very active in the game.

What a thrill it was for me to compete with the likes of Ben Hogan and Sam Snead. I can still vividly remember the excitement I felt every time I had a chance to play with them or even just watch them practice.

But I also cherish the many happy hours I spent listening to players like Tommy Bolt and Gene Sarazen as they shared their wonderful stories and recollections in locker rooms after we had finished our rounds. Can you imagine what it was like for me to hear stories about people like Walter Hagen and Bobby Jones told by people who knew them personally and, in some cases, competed against them? They are some of my fondest memories. In fact, every year as the Masters approaches, I look forward to the Champions Dinner so I can catch up with old friends and hear their stories.

Today, of course, the shoe is on the other foot. After all these years, competing around the world, I am the one who is able to share my stories of friends like Jack Nicklaus and Arnold Palmer with a new generation of golfers. And I can tell you that they are most appreciative and interested.

I am delighted that Don Wade asked me to write this Foreword for his latest collection of golf anecdotes. Reading these books reminds me of the happy hours I spent with some of the best storytellers of all time, and they bring back many fond and happy memories. I love these books and know you will enjoy this latest in the series. I don't think they will lower your scores, but I'm sure they will increase your enjoyment of this great game. And remember, "The harder you practice, the luckier you get."

—Gary Player

ACKNOWLEDGMENTS

If there's one thing I've learned in a lifetime of playing golf, it's that the breaks pretty much even out. Certainly, this series of books, which began with *"And Then Jack Said to Arnie . . ."* in 1991, has been one of the biggest breaks of my professional career. This is the tenth in the series and to the extent they've been successful, I have a lot of people to thank.

First, thanks to the incomparable Paul Szep, who has done the brilliant illustrations for the series. For the last thirty-plus years, Szeppy labored as an editorial cartoonist for the *Boston Globe*, where he was one of the best in the business. Don't just take my word for it. He has two Pulitzer prizes to prove it. He left the *Globe* in 2001 to pursue other adventures. With any luck, his work may soon be appearing in a paper near you.

Here's a nod to Steve Szurlez, my old friend from our days at *Golf Digest*, where he has been the senior photographer for longer than either of us would care to remember. He's captured the spirit of these books and of the game itself in his cover photos. They make clear why he's among the best in the business, too.

The extraordinarily patient Matthew Carnicelli took over as my editor when the sainted Nancy Crossman left Contemporary Books to start her own literary agency. Like Nancy, Matthew has been a friend, cheerleader, and a wise and understanding critic. Through five books he's maintained his sense of humor and enthusiasm, and for that, thanks. And thanks as well to John Nolan, Contemporary's publisher for all of the above, and Craig Bolt, project editor extraordinaire.

Every writer needs and deserves a loyal agent to guide him or her through the shoals of a writing career. I've been luckier than most. Chris Tomasino was my first agent and she helped launch this series. She handed me off to Jonathan Diamond when she struck out on her own, and a few years later, when he fled New York for California, Jennifer Unter inherited me. For that, I am extremely grateful. Thanks to all three of you, and to Bob Rosen as well. It was Bob who suggested doing the original book, and I thank him for all the help and guidance over the years.

Thanks as well to all my friends in the game who have been so generous in sharing their stories. These books would not have been possible without their kindness.

And last, but certainly not least, thanks to my wife, Julia, and our three great kids, Ben, Darcy, and Andy, for their patience, support, and love.

You guys are the best, and this one's for you.

"And Then Justin Told Sergio..."

AMY ALCOTT

A writer asked Amy Alcott how the LPGA had changed from her early days in the 1970s until today.

"When I started out, you'd finish your round and have a scotch or two with some of the other players," Alcott said. "Today, if you run into another player after your round, you give them a Power Bar and a glass of carrot juice."

AUGUSTA NATIONAL GOLF CLUB

Jack Nicklaus won the Masters six times but until 1998—thirty-five years after his first victory—he never owned a Green Jacket of his own.

In 1963, when he won his first Masters, Masters officials grabbed a 46 long off the rack and watched as Arnold Palmer placed it on the new champion. It was a touching moment, but the jacket was acres too large.

When he returned the next year, the club had somehow forgotten to have a jacket made for him, so he borrowed the jacket owned by Thomas E. Dewey, the former New York governor who lost to Harry Truman in the 1948 presidential election. He continued to wear Dewey's Green Jacket until 1972. By that time, it was looking a bit on the seedy side so Nicklaus had Hart, Schaffner and Marx—his longtime clothing company—make up a jacket.

It was the wrong material and the wrong color, although it did fit nicely.

So Nicklaus continued to borrow jackets from other members until 1997 when he finally told the club's chairman, Jack Stephens, who ordered Nicklaus to be fitted for a jacket.

By that time, Nicklaus was too amused by it all to finally relent. But when he arrived in 1999 Stephens insisted he had to undergo a fitting—no ifs, ands, or buts.

Even Jack Nicklaus knows when the game is over. He finally got his very own size 44 regular.

When Clifford Roberts was running the show at Augusta National, there was a board of governors that existed for no apparent reason.

One year Roberts began a board meeting by asking Charlie Yates, the club secretary, what was on the agenda.

"Why, nothing, Cliff," he said.

At yet another meeting, he asked Yates to distribute the minutes.

"This year's, last year's or next year's?" Yates asked.

The Masters, as we know it today, very nearly didn't get off the ground. When Cliff Roberts and Bob Jones first proposed the tournament to the membership, many objected to losing four days of play. As a compromise, Roberts arranged with the PGA of America to keep the size of the field small enough so members could play in the morning and the pros in the afternoon.

Clifford Roberts was surprisingly open to suggestions that he believed might improve either Augusta National or the Masters.

For over a year Roberts toyed with the idea of sending a scorer out with each twosome. The scorer would wear a large hat that would display the twosome's scores so the gallery could easily keep track of how each group stood.

Fortunately, he lost interest in the idea, just as he did years later when someone suggested that the runner-up be given a green vest.

While someone might be flattered if Roberts took his suggestion to heart, there was often a kicker. Take the case of Mr. Clarence J. Schoo.

In the early days of the club, there was a small creek that ran along the base of the hill in the first fairway. Schoo constantly drove into the creek and often complained to his friend Cliff Roberts.

Finally Roberts relented and had the creek filled in. And then he had the bill sent to Clarence J. Schoo.

Mr. Schoo was quite a character and apparently had a generous nature.

One day he was playing the course and hit an absolutely awful shot. He turned to his caddie, who was new on the job but had already heard stories about the infamous Mr. Schoo's golf game.

"I must be the worst golfer in this club," he said in despair.

"Oh no, sir," the caddie said. "Mr. Schoo is the worst golfer in this club."

Augusta National is a golf club. There are no tennis courts. There are no paddle tennis courts. And most important of all, there is no swimming pool—largely because Cliff Roberts detested the idea.

One evening Roberts was talking to Jack Stephens, who went on to become the club's chairman, about building a new cottage. Stephens agreed to underwrite it immediately with one condition.

"I told him I love to swim and I'd like to have a pool built under the cabin," Stephens recalled. "He was appalled. He hated the idea but I kept at him. I didn't want anything to do with a pool. I just wanted to win an argument with him since I never had. Finally he gave in. As soon as he did, I told him I didn't care a damn about the pool. He was a very relieved man."

Clifford Roberts was very particular about his playing partners, particularly when there was a little money riding on the competition.

One day a new assistant pro, Robert Barrett, was drafted to join Roberts's foursome. While understandably nervous, he played very well, parring the first nine holes. When he putted out on the 9th green, Roberts said, "Bob, we don't need any more pars. What we need are birdies. Why don't you go back into the shop and send out someone who can make some birdies?"

Barrett thought Roberts was kidding.

He wasn't.

One day Charlie Yates, a longtime member at Augusta National and a former British Amateur champion, arrived at the course in shorts. Roberts looked at him sternly.

"Charlie, what do you have planned for today?" Roberts asked.

Yates told him he planned to play golf.

"Where?" Roberts asked.

Roberts was a meticulous dresser and it always bothered him that he couldn't find golf shirts that fit him properly. Smalls were too small and mediums were too big.

"What I need is a small-medium, but no one makes them," Roberts said.

As luck would have it, one of his friends knew someone who owned a shirt factory and arranged to have a special run of shirts made just for Roberts.

Of course, the factory had to shut down all other production to make the shirts for Mr. Roberts.

AUSSIE RULES

An American writer was visiting Melbourne for the 1988 World Cup matches at Royal Melbourne. As luck would have it, Melbourne is home to some of the world's finest courses and, happily, some of the world's friendliest people.

A day or so into his visit, he was invited to play one of the local courses by some fellow writers. From the first hole on, his partner took great pains to give him advice on how to play each hole. As they prepared to tee off on a short, uphill par 4, his Australian host pointed to a small mound at the top of the hill.

"That's what we call the Nipple," he said. "Reach that and you're home free of worries."

SEVE BALLESTEROS

Seve Ballesteros won the 1979 British Open at Royal Lytham & St. Annes, beating Ben Crenshaw and Jack Nicklaus by three strokes.

Nine years later he returned to the club for the 108th British Open. When he entered the locker room he found that he had been assigned locker number 108. He also found a note.

"Welcome back, Seve," the note read. "We know you'll win again."

Seve found out who wrote the note and sought the man out.

"Thank you," he said to the man. "I will win this week."

And he did.

Seve's victory in the 1988 British Open was his third and, in likelihood, final win in the game's oldest championship. One day he was asked to reflect on his record.

"Winning the Open is very difficult," Seve said. "Winning it again is very difficult. Winning it three times is something magical, don't you think?"

Seve Ballesteros has been an enormous force in the success of the European team in recent Ryder Cup history, both as a player and as the captain of the victorious 1997 team in the matches at Valderrama Golf Club.

Ballesteros was intensely involved in every aspect of the matches, even to the point where he was criticized by some of his players—but not fellow countryman Ignacio Garcia.

"Every time I was puzzled and thinking 'What should I do now?' Seve would suddenly appear as if by magic," Garcia said. "He would calm me down and tell me what to do. We had our hands on the clubs, but Seve is the one who hit the shots."

In his prime, Seve Ballesteros was a tremendously aggressive player, knowing he could take uncanny risks because of his phenomenal short game. He was a particularly daring putter.

One time, early in his career, a writer asked him to translate "Lag putt" into Spanish.

Seve pondered the question for several moments.

"What is a lag putt?" he asked.

Seve was one of the first Spanish players to make an impact on American golf. Naturally, the language difference did result in some humorous moments.

He played in his first U.S. Open in 1978 at Cherry Hills Country Club. He was already a phenomenon and prior to the first round was brought to the interview room to face the press corps.

"Ladies and gentlemen, we have Steve Ballesteros from Spain," a USGA official announced.

"It's Seve," one of the writers called out.

"No, it's Steve," the USGA official insisted.

Seve turned twenty-one during the 1978 Masters and the galleries would often sing "Happy Birthday" to him as he walked past.

An American writer was following Ballesteros in the company of Spanish journalist Nuria Pastor. When Seve walked past them, the American writer offered a birthday greeting of his own.

"Feliz Navidad," the American said.

"Thank you very much," said Seve.

The American was very pleased with himself.

"How'd I do," he asked Pastor. "Did I pronounce it okay?"

"Beautifully," Pastor said. "You just wished him a Merry Christmas."

Seve began playing golf as a seven-year-old. He found an old 3-iron head and stuck it on the end of a stick. He would walk along the beach hitting pebbles with his makeshift club.

He began caddying when he was eight and his brother Manuel, by then a professional, gave him a real 3-iron.

Armed with his new club and balls he found scouring the Real Pedrena course, he would sneak onto the course in the darkness of night and hit balls for hours.

"When you hit the balls you could not see where they landed so you had to turn your head and listen very hard for the way the ball sounded when it hit the ground," Seve remembered. "The softer the sound the better. Those were the ones that landed on the fairways."

One of the more colorful collaborations in golf was the pairing of Seve Ballesteros with Mac O'Grady, the former Tour pro turned swing guru. To say they are both colorful and strong-willed individuals is a colossal understatement.

During the 1994 U.S. Open at Oakmont, the two were leaving the course when O'Grady ran into a golf writer and immediately began to engage him in a discussion of one weighty matter or another. Seve waited patiently for several minutes and then he lost interest.

While Mac chattered on, Ballesteros produced a baby's pacifier and put it in O'Grady's mouth.

"This is the only way to shut him up," Ballesteros said.

O'Grady, with the pacifier still in his mouth, got in Ballestero's car and they drove away.

PATTY BERG

Throughout her Hall of Fame career, Patty Berg has been nothing if not the picture of determination—a trait that surfaced early in her life.

In 1933, young Patty entered the Minneapolis City Ladies' Championship and quickly discovered, as Bob Jones often said, the difference between golf and tournament golf. She shot a 122 in the medal round and then was trounced in her first match in the last flight.

"I don't think I won a single hole," she recalled years later. "I was shattered. As I walked back to the clubhouse I vowed that I would spend every single one of the next 365 days trying to improve. I thought that if I could shoot better than 122 in the medal round and maybe move up a flight that would be a great thing. As it turned out, the next year I was the medallist and won the championship, which proves that if you really set your mind to something and work hard you can succeed."

BETHPAGE PARK
BLACK COURSE

Bethpage State Park on New York's Long Island has five courses, but the Black course, which hosts the 2002 U.S. Open, is by far the most famous—and with good reason.

The course was designed by the legendary architect A. W. Tillinghast, who also designed, among other courses, the two courses at Winged Foot, Quaker Ridge, and the Upper and Lower courses at Baltusrol.

The course will play about 7,300 yards for the Open, and while it plays shorter for everyday play, it remains so formidable a test that players are greeted with a warning sign: "WARNING! the Black course is an extremely difficult course, which we recommend for highly skilled golfers only."

Still, people flock to the course, literally arriving in the middle of the night to line up for starting times. And the greens fee is one of the greatest bargains in the game: a mere $18.

So how tough is the Black course?

A few years after it opened in 1936, Sam Snead and Byron Nelson visited for an exhibition.

Sam walked off after fifteen holes. He'd seen enough.

TOMMY BOLT

Tommy Bolt took Arnold Palmer under his wing when the kid from Latrobe came out on Tour in 1955.

"That boy was so young that Old Tom had to teach him everything I knew," Bolt jokes. "The first thing I had to teach him is that you always throw the clubs ahead of you, not behind. Saves a lot of wear and tear on your caddie, don't you see?"

As luck would have it, Bolt was paired with Palmer in the final round of the 1955 Canadian Open, as Palmer was on his way to his first PGA Tour title. As Palmer remembers, everything was going along just fine until the 6th hole.

"I had, I don't know, a six or seven shot lead and I hooked my drive into the trees," Palmer says. "All the way from the tee to my ball, Tommy's telling me to just play it safe and pitch the ball back into the fairway. He was being very precise, just to make sure I understood what I was supposed to do. By the time I got to the ball, I was sort of laughing at him, and when I studied the shot, I saw there was a small opening between the trees. I took a 6-iron and knocked it up through the trees and onto the green. I looked over at Tommy and I thought he was going to have a heart attack. He wouldn't talk to me for the rest of the round."

Tommy Bolt didn't waste any time on the golf course and didn't have much patience with guys who did.

One day he was paired with Jack Nicklaus, who had just joined the Tour. Nicklaus races between shots but is very deliberate once it's his turn to play.

"Jack will walk you to death," Lee Trevino once observed.

Bolt is just the opposite. He strides majestically down the fairways and then, once he reaches the ball, pulls the trigger without a lot of attention to detail.

One year the two were paired at a tournament at Westchester Country Club. After watching Jack line up his shot and then back away, Tommy said to the gallery, "How long does this kid take to play?"

When Jack backed off again Bolt said to his caddie, "If the kid doesn't hit, I will." Again, the gallery cracked up.

After Nicklaus hit his drive, Bolt sauntered to the tee and hit his drive as though he didn't have a care in the world—to applause from the gallery.

Tommy Bolt has always given Ben Hogan a lot of credit for his success.

"In 1955 my game was just in terrible shape," Bolt recalls. "I was fighting a hook and losing more often than I was winning. I asked Ben for some help and he told me to come to Fort Worth for a couple weeks during the off-season. He worked with me changing how I gripped the club with my left hand. I had it in a pretty strong position and he weakened it.

"'Don't tell the kids,' Ben said. 'They won't appreciate it.'"

"I stayed there for a couple weeks practicing at Colonial, and Ben used to hide in the bushes watching me to make sure I was doing it right," Bolt said. "Every so often he'd correct me. By the time I was finished, I had taken the left side of the hole out of play. For the first time I had so much confidence in my game."

Bolt won the 1958 Colonial National Invitation and went to Southern Hills Country Club filled with confidence. His game was in good shape. Colonial was a course very similar to Southern Hills, and while the other players complained about the heat and humidity and the thick Bermuda rough, Bolt was very comfortable, having been raised in Shreveport, Louisiana.

Indeed, he was so confident that when he birdied the first hole in the opening round, he said to himself "My, my, I wonder who's going to finish second this week?"

There wasn't much money on the Tour in Bolt's early days, so he kept his bank account solvent by playing high-stakes matches. One of his favorite places was Hot Springs, Arkansas, a place that has always welcomed those willing to wager with open arms.

"I used to have a regular pigeon named Louis Marrow," Bolt remembers fondly. "He had a chain of successful furniture stores and a drinking problem, which was bad for him but fortunate for me. He'd come to Hot Springs to take the cure and dry out. He loved to play golf and gamble but he couldn't hit the ground with his hat, don'tcha see. We'd play $1,500 nassaus, which was a ton of money back then. I'd give him about a million strokes and we'd go at it. The last match we ever played was a beauty. He had a two-footer for all the money and he started getting the shakes so bad the putter fell out of his hands. Easiest money I ever made."

The hardest money Bolt ever made came in 1950. He was driving to a tournament in North Carolina when his 1941 Nash broke down and died. Bolt was completely broke, so he was reduced to taking a job at a driving range in Chapel Hill giving lessons for three dollars an hour.

"Let me tell you something, pards," Bolt says. "Teaching golf to the uncoordinated is the hardest job in the world."

Tommy Bolt struggled with money for much of his early years.

He started caddying as a thirteen-year-old, earning fifty cents a bag per round. He fell in love with the game almost immediately and eagerly looked forward to Mondays—"Caddie Day" when he could play all day long. There was only one catch: before a caddie could play he had to present four golf balls to the caddiemaster. This meant getting up before dawn, often on bitterly cold winter days, and wading barefoot through the course's ponds and creeks in search of balls.

Before he turned pro, he entered as many amateur events as he could. He couldn't take cash prizes, but he could sell his prizes.

"Man, I'd find out what they were giving away and I'd play for whatever I could get the most money for," Bolt said. "One time the prize for third place was a set of irons. I had a buyer for those little beauties before I even teed off. The problem was playing bad enough to finish third."

THE BOYS

Every club in America probably has some variation of "The Boys." They are the backbone of the place, playing more golf than anyone else, and enjoy the club as a home away from home—whichever club they happen to be at that day. To be one of The Boys, it helps to work on some variation of Wall Street, since a fair amount of disposable income is preferable, as is an expense account. It also helps if you're single or, failing that, have an unusually understanding wife.

For The Boys, the ideal club would have a very good golf course, a men's locker room with an attendant who doesn't do too much damage, at least one bar, and plenty of beer available on the course. A grillroom is also useful, preferably a men's grill—modern politically correct thinking notwithstanding. Things like swimming pools, ladies' locker rooms, and—horror of horrors—children's summer camp programs are unnecessary at best and a plague on civilization at worst.

My friend Dennis Powell is the leader of The Boys at our club. It is a role he was born to and cherishes.

"We used to go on these road trips for tournaments," Dennis recalls fondly. "One tournament was called 'The Aldo.' It was named after a guy named Aldo who ran into a little financial trouble and wound up scooting out of town owing everyone money. He even owed his club money. We played the tournament there in his honor. The only requirement for entry was that Aldo had to have beaten you out of at least $100. We'd begin the day by having a few pops just to loosen up, and then we'd tee off around eleven-thirty. You got a stroke for every beer you drank during the round. That took care of any stiffs that snuck in. It leveled the field because even the good golfers were usually useless by the end of the day. After the round we'd go to this joint named the Hilltop and you'd pull your partner's name out of a hat, match scores, and split up the prize money.

"One year we played the Aldo on Halloween," Dennis continued. "We called it the 'Hallow-Aldo.' Everyone had to wear a costume. One guy showed up in a devil costume. I came as Spuds McKenzie. Timmy Cassidy showed up with a blood-hound mask on. The starter looked at him and asked him if he was part of the tournament. Timmy said 'No, I always wear this when I play golf.'

"Another year we finished playing and we were drinking at the Hilltop when my wife called and told me that I had to come home because our house had been robbed.

"Is the guy still there?" I asked her.

"'No, the dogs chased him off,' she said.

"Then there's no point in me coming home and ruining my day," I said. "We're watching Notre Dame play Southern Cal. I'll be back after the game."

At this point, Dennis's wife put a policeman on the phone. The officer told Dennis he had to come home to sign some forms.

"I'm not coming," Dennis said. "You guys already missed him and I have a better chance of catching him here when he tries to sell the stuff out of his car."

"We used to go up to The Concord, the big Jewish resort in the Catskills," Dennis explained. "Since we're all Irish, we'd think up these Jewish-sounding names so we'd fit right in. One guy was Lippy Kuppman, because he was always lipping out putts. Another guy was Jason Shanker, because he was always getting these bad cases of the shanks. I think I was Hy Gross one year, because I wasn't scoring that well. The only problem with The Concord was that they didn't have a lot of big beer drinkers up there very often. We went up one Friday, played and then stayed up most of the night drinking. The next day we went out to play and we had completely wiped out their beer supply. We had to go out to a local store and stock up before we could play.

"Anyway, they used to have a starter there named Chicago," Dennis continued. "He watched us tee off. We all hit these big drives and he comes over to me and he whispers, 'Hey, you guys ain't Jewish are you?'

"'How could you tell?' I asked him.

"'The red faces and the case of Michelob on each cart,' Chicago said."

It's not a requirement that The Boys have to belong to more than one club, but it helps.

23

"You never want to belong to just one club," Dennis Powell explained. "You need to have a few back-ups in case you get tossed out of your regular club."

Like everyone, age eventually takes its toll on The Boys. "One day we were trying out these new drivers," Dennis Powell recalls. "Finally I said the hell with it. 'Let's get out of here. We're wasting our time. Our bodies are falling apart faster than they can improve these clubs.'"

"I went to a new doctor and he gave me a bunch of pills for all the stuff that's wrong with me," Dennis Powell remembered. "I had a pill for my blood pressure; one for my gout; another one for Lyme disease; a pill I was supposed to take for high pressure situations; and a high-powered sleeping pill that I was never to take with alcohol. This one day Tony Abbott and I are playing a twenty-seven-hole tournament, so I figured I better take my pills. The problem is that I took the sleeping pill by mistake. By about the 3rd hole I was chopping the ball around and laughing uncontrollably. On the 6th green I started to walk backwards to line up my putt, lost my balance, and backpedaled right off into the shrubs. It was the third nine before I got my game back. It was a disaster."

CADDIES

An American came to St. Andrews and was lucky enough to get a starting time on The Old Course. He hit a good drive on the opening hole, but hit his second shot fat, gouging a huge divot from the turf.

"Aye, sir," his old caddie said. "The Good Lord made The Old Course. I don't think he'd appreciate you placing some new bunkers about the place. You'll see we have quite enough as it is."

A caddie at the Royal Liverpool Golf Club named Reg Barton began caddying in 1930 and closed his career by caddying for Prince Andrew, the Duke of York. When a friend told him that the Prince might be visiting the club for a round of golf, Reg's memory kicked into high gear.

"If you see the Prince, would you ask him for my pencil?" Reg said. "He never gave it back to me the last time he was here."

An American was playing The Old Course at St. Andrews and right from the beginning, he and his caddie didn't get along. They argued about club selection and the break of the putts and anything else that came up. At the end of the round, the American grudgingly paid his caddie.

"You must be the worst caddie in the world," the American said.

"Not bloody likely," the caddie said. "That would be too great a coincidence."

Jerry Pate was dueling Tom Weiskopf and John Mahaffey in the final round of the 1976 U.S. Open at the Atlanta Athletic Club.

A former U.S. Amateur Champion, Pate was in his rookie year on Tour and was understandably nervous given the pressure of trying to win the Open. Not as nervous, however, as his caddie, John.

"We were standing on the tee waiting to play, and I felt this burning on my hand. I thought I'd been stung or something, but when I looked down John was burning my hand with his cigarette. In a funny way it helped me because it broke the tension."

A group was preparing to tee off at one of the more exclusive clubs in the New York City area.

As they stood on the tee, one of their caddies arrived and introduced himself. Then he handed one of the players his driver.

He hit his first ball out of bounds.

He hit his second ball out of bounds.

He hit his third ball out of bounds and handed his driver back to the caddie.

"You're the worst ******* caddie I've ever had," he said.

My friend Tony Abbott loves to play golf in Scotland. One of his favorite caddies is a postman from Gullane who loops at Muirfield. One day Tony asked him which visitors are the best to caddy for.

"Well, I love Yanks because they're very generous when it comes time to pay," the caddie said. "I'm a Scot, so naturally I hate the Brits. The Germans and the French are hard to take. Just the other day I thought I was in for a big payday from this Yank, but once he paid me I realized he was a Canadian."

"Every year when we go to Scotland we make a point of playing Turnberry," Tony Abbott recalls. "We team two Americans with two Scots. I always put a pint of lager in my bag and when we reach the 7th hole, I pull out the beer and give my caddie a pound. On this day, I handed my caddie the beer on the first tee.

"Mate, are you the pound-lager Yank?" the caddie asked in gleeful anticipation.

One year Jack Nicklaus was playing an exhibition match at The Greenbrier, the magnificent resort in the West Virginia mountains.

As he prepared to hit his second shot on one of the par 5s, he checked the yardage with his caddie. His shot came up short, landing in a bunker.

"Are you sure of that yardage?" he said to the caddie.

"Mr. Jack, I just gave you the mileage," the caddie said. "I didn't tell you whether to take the bus or the Volkswagen."

A Thai woman named Yupa Poosorn caddied for Australia's Rodney Pampling in the 2000 Johnny Walker Classic in Bangkok. As luck would have it, Pampling was paired with Tiger Woods in the third round, which was an answer to Ms. Poosorn's prayers—literally. She had promised the gods that she would offer up two chickens if she was somehow able to meet Woods, whose mother is Thai. When Woods came to the first tee he introduced himself to her, marveling at her ability to carry such a large golf bag. Naturally, this encounter with the world's most famous athlete was a thrill beyond words.

"I promised the spirit that if I can ever meet Tiger Woods again, I will give it a whole pig," she said.

No man has ever received a greater honor.

A visiting golfer hit his third shot into the infamous bunker guarding the front of the green on the Road Hole at St. Andrews. It was just the latest calamity in what had already been sixteen holes of misery.

"What do I do now?" he asked his caddie.

"Well, sir, the Jigger Inn isn't too far from here," the caddie said. "I think we should go over, have a wee one, and rethink the whole bloody thing."

In the 1995 British Open at St. Andrews, Jack Nicklaus hit his drive into the notorious "Hell Bunker" on the 14th hole and wound up making a 10 on the hole.

A few years later, an American visitor was playing The Old Course and as he stood on the 14th tee, he asked his caddie if he could "carry the bunker."

"I doubt it, sir," the caddie said. "The beast must weigh twenty tons."

The final holes of The Players Championship were the stage for some of the most dramatic moments of the 2000 PGA Tour season.

Hal Sutton held a three-stroke lead over Tiger Woods coming to the reachable, par-5 16th. Minutes later, after Woods eagled the hole, Sutton's lead was cut to one stroke, which is where things stood as the two players reached the 18th tee.

It is in moments like this that a caddie can either really help a player or hurt him. In this case, Sutton's caddie, Freddie Burns, got the job done.

"Hal, who's the best damn driver of the golf ball in the whole damned world?" Burns said.

"I am," Sutton said.

"Damn right you are," Burns said. "Now you just bust that driver right on past Tiger's ball and we'll be in the driver's seat."

Sure enough, Sutton's drive carried past Woods's 2-iron tee shot, and after Woods missed the green with his second shot, Sutton drilled a 6-iron eight feet from the hole, matched Woods's par, and won by a stroke—one of the few times anyone beat Tiger Woods head-to-head in 2000.

"You guys were the best—this week," Woods told Burns after the round.

A man was playing Pine Valley for the first time and it wasn't a pretty sight. His caddie struggled through the round and had managed to keep a civil tongue in his head until the final hole. After another poor drive, the man pitched the ball back into the fairway.

"What do you think?" he asked his caddie. "Can I get there with a 7-iron?"

"Sooner or later," said his caddie.

A man hit his drive deep into the woods, and the caddies headed in to try and find the ball. After searching for several minutes, one of the kids found it and called to the player.

"Here it is, sir," he said. "Titleist 3."

When the man reached the ball, he bent over and looked at it.

"Sorry, this isn't mine," he said. "Mine is a new ball."

"It was when we started, sir," the caddie said. "But we've been out here a long time."

For many years, Massachusetts's infamous "Blue Laws" banned golf on Sundays. When the law was changed to allow golf, some people still had some concerns.

"What do you think?" a member asked his caddie midway through the round. "Is it a sin to play golf on the Sabbath?"

"No sir," said the caddie. "But the way we're playing is a crime."

After hitting another drive out of bounds, a man turned to his playing partner and apologized.

"I just want you to know that this isn't my usual game," he said.

"I wonder what game he usually plays," one caddie whispered to the other.

After getting off to a truly horrible start, a golfer managed to make back-to-back bogeys.

"How do you like my game now, boy?" he said to his caddie as they walked to the next tee.

"Splendid, sir," the caddie said. "It sort of reminds me of golf."

Nearing the end of a frustrating and disappointing round, a golfer tried to make amends to his caddie.

"I swear, I've never played this badly before," he said.

"You mean you've played before?" the caddie replied.

Gary Player came to the final green in the 1978 Masters needing to make a fifteen-foot birdie putt to lock up a tournament record round of 64 and, in all probability, a victory, and the greatest comeback in Masters history. As he approached the green his caddie, Eddie McCorey, gave him one last pep talk.

"Boss, we've got to win," he said. "I need to buy a house."

For many years in the prime of his career, Angelo Argea caddied for Jack Nicklaus. One day, after being paired with Nicklaus for several rounds, Johnny Miller asked Argea an interesting question that prompted an even more interesting answer.

"Angelo, you really don't do much for Jack do you? I mean, you don't do yardages. You don't club him. You don't chart the course and you hardly ever read a green, but he still pays you $1,500 a week, which is more than anyone else pays. You must do something special. What is it?"

Argea thought about it for a moment.

"Jack only wants me to do a few things," he said. "First, I always wish him good luck early in the round. When things aren't going well, he wants me to remind him that he's the greatest player in the world. Finally, he wants me to remind him that there are plenty of holes left to play."

"That's it?" an incredulous Miller asked.

"That's it," Angelo said. "But I do it very well."

JOANNE CARNER

JoAnne Carner is one of the greatest and most popular players in the history of the LPGA. Along with her obvious
skills, she also possesses a wonderful sense of humor—particularly when it comes to poking fun at herself.

In the early 1980s the LPGA was marketing itself, at least
in some small part, on the sexuality of players such as Jan
Stephenson, Kathy Young, Muffin Spencer-Devlin, and others. When Carner learned that she was going to be featured
as well, she was delighted.

"It's a victory for cellulite around the world," she crowed.

Carner was the captain of the 1994 United States Solheim
Cup team, and at the players' dinner that opened the
competition, her comic timing was again on display. Beth
Daniel, one of the team's veterans, rose to speak and
reminded her teammates that "it's not over until the fat lady
holds the cup."

"What?" Carner roared, to the delight of the crowd.

CHARLIE COE

Charlie Coe was one of America's top amateurs, winning the 1949 and '58 U.S. Amateurs and losing to Jack Nicklaus, 1-up, in 1959.

On his way to the finals of the 1949 Amateur at Oak Hill Country Club's East course, he beat Bill Campbell, who would go on to serve as president of the USGA and captain of the R&A, 8 & 7. Then in the finals against Rufus King, he was four under par for the final twenty-three holes and made eight 3s in the twenty-six holes it took for him to win, 11 & 10.

Coe was modest and soft-spoken, and he tried to attribute his victory to luck. At least one newspaperman wasn't buying it.

"Yeah, lucky like Babe Ruth, Joe Louis, Man O' War, and Ben Hogan," he said.

HARRY COOPER

Harry Cooper might well be the best player who never won a major championship.

Cooper, an Englishman by birth who was raised in Texas, won thirty-one PGA Tour events, which placed him thirteenth on the Tour's all-time victory list at the time of his death in 2000 at the age of ninety-six.

He led the 1927 U.S. Open at Oakmont Country Club until Tommy Armour, the last player who could catch him, sank a fifteen-footer on the 72nd hole to tie him. In the following day's playoff, he led Armour by a stroke as they played the 15th hole—only to watch Armour run in a fifty-footer for birdie. On the 16th, a par 3, he made a double bogey and fell two strokes behind.

Nine years later, Cooper bogeyed the 14th, 15th, and 18th holes at Baltusrol's Upper course and still managed to set a seventy-two-hole scoring record of 284. Unfortunately, however, Tony Manero rallied to beat him by a stroke.

By this time, Cooper had come to expect the worst. Earlier in the year he had led the Masters for the first three rounds, but shot a perfectly respectable 76 in the driving rain in the morning of the final round.

"Horton Smith (who won the inaugural Masters in 1934) went out in brilliant sunshine in the afternoon and shot a 72 to beat me by a stroke," Cooper recalled later. "Even the weather was against me."

Cooper's negative thinking mystified even his closest friends.

"Coopy was a magnificent shotmaker," recalls two-time PGA Champion Paul Runyan. "I would rank him with Bobby Jones and Byron Nelson as the three best fairway wood players I ever saw. But unfortunately, he was also the most pessimistic, negative thinker I have ever known. He truly believed that the other fellows got all the breaks and he never got any. Off the course, he was one of the most magnificent human beings you could ever hope to meet."

Ben Hogan certainly agreed.

For decades, people have debated the nature of Hogan's famous "Secret" that allowed him to transform himself from a struggling professional to one of the game's greatest champions. Certainly part of the credit was owed to Harry Cooper.

"Ben had a terrible hook, which caused him to play well for a period of time, but would jump up and kill him under pressure—usually in the final round," Cooper recalled. "I noticed that because he had a very long backswing, he would let go of the club with the last one or two fingers of his left hand at the top of his swing. That forced him to regrip the club on the downswing. You can't do that. I took him aside and told him I thought that if he fixed that one flaw, he'd be a much better player. I don't know if that was his secret, but I do know that whenever he saw me in later years, he always gave me a hug."

Incidentally, Cooper so loved teaching that he was giving lessons at Westchester Country Club outside New York City until he was ninety-three—making him the oldest active PGA professional at the time.

THE COUNTRY CLUB

The Country Club, in the Boston suburb of Brookline, is one of the most historic sites in American golf and also a bastion of Yankee propriety. So it was with a certain horror that one evening a member out for his postdinner constitutional came across a couple engaged in a fairly vigorous bout of lovemaking out among the historic green and bunkers of the 17th hole of the Open course.

"See here, young man," he snorted. "You can't do that here."

"Why not," the man said. "We're not bothering anyone."

"Well, for one thing, it's where Francis [Ouimet] won the Open, and for another, you're not a member," he replied, quite rightly.

DEAR OLD DAD

Tiger Woods has always been particularly close to his father, Earl, who often accompanied young Tiger to tournaments. But as Tiger grew older and more mature, his father sensed that his son didn't require quite as much parental attention.

"One day in 2000, Tiger and I were playing at a course in Newport Beach and I asked him if he wanted me to be around more than I had been," Earl Woods said. "Tiger looked at me and said, 'I'll be all right, Pop.' That's when I knew he was grown up and I had done my job."

Bobby Jones was very attached to his father, "The Colonel," and his father was, by every account, a supportive and understanding dad.

In 1913, when Jones was just eleven, he shot an 80 at East Lake. As soon as the last putt dropped, he raced across the course to find his father. After watching him putt out, he approached and held the scorecard out for his father.

"He looked at the card, then looked at me," Jones remembered. "Then he reached out and gave me a big hug, a very hard hug. I don't remember what he said, or even if he said anything, but I'll never forget that hug."

By every account, Jack Nicklaus is every bit as good a father as he is a golfer. Still, that didn't mean he cut the kids any slack when it came to competition.

"Jack would go out and play against the kids, and trust me, everyone knew exactly how the matches stood," recalls his wife, Barbara. "I can't count the times he'd come to the last hole needing to sink a putt for a birdie to win. He'd look at whatever kid it was and say something like "I hate to do this to you but . . ." and then he'd sink the putt. It drove them crazy. He'd even do it to me when we played."

Jack Nicklaus had a very special relationship with his father, Charlie, and was devastated by his death.

When he was asked what one event he wished his father had lived to see, he said it was the ceremony honoring him at the 2000 Memorial Tournament.

"If dad had been here it would have meant I would have had him with me for the last thirty years and he wouldn't have missed a thing," Nicklaus said.

Charlie Nicklaus was understandably proud of his son, and often pointed out that it was an ankle injury he suffered that forced him to take up golf and introduced young Jack to the game he would grow up to dominate.

"My dad always loved telling that story," Nicklaus once said. "I'm sure if there's anyone up in Heaven willing to listen, he's still telling it."

Jack Nicklaus played in the 1959 Walker Cup matches at Muirfield and his father and two of his friends made the trip over. They decided that since they were there, they might as well play the The Old Course at St. Andrews.

When they returned to Muirfield, they told young Jack that it was the worst course they had ever seen.

"Of course, it could have been because dad three-putted fifteen greens and his two friends weren't much better," Nicklaus recalls.

Patty Sheehan's father, Bobo, was a tremendous athlete. He coached the 1956 U.S. Olympic Men's Alpine team and also coached football, baseball, skiing, and golf at Middlebury College, in Vermont.

Like her father, Patty proved to also be a wonderful athlete. In her youth, she was a very successful skier, winning a national title at age eleven.

By the time she was thirteen, however, she wanted to give up skiing but dreaded telling her father, who held out such hope for her future. Finally, she broke the news to him.

"That's fine with me, Patty," he said. "I've spent enough time freezing out on the slopes. Why should you have to?"

Nancy Lopez learned to play golf from her father, Domingo, who has always been her biggest supporter and greatest fan. Whenever she found herself in a slump, she would call home and her father would cure the problem from long distance, usually with a piece of advice that was at once breathtakingly simple and yet often profound.

At one point in her career, she went through a stretch where she couldn't buy a putt. Her fellow players offered all sorts of advice, which only made matters worse. Finally, she called her father and began explaining all the different things she was working on.

"Nancy," he said. "Don't think about all these things. They only confuse you. When you putt, the ball has eyes. That is all you need to remember."

Sure enough, the slump ended as mysteriously as it began. Thanks, dad.

DISASTERS

One David Ayton was leading the 1885 British Open at St. Andrews by five strokes as he approached the 17th green. What happened next was worthy of a "B" movie.

Facing a short pitch to the green, he hit the ball into the deep pot bunker guarding the front of the green. His next shot rocketed over the green and came to rest on the nearby road. The following shot rolled across the green and back into the bunker. He failed to escape the bunker with either of his next two shots, finally reaching the green in nine, and then two-putted for the 11 that left him six strokes out of the lead.

People have quit the game for less.

Ian Woosnam of Wales began the final round of the 2001 British Open just one stroke off the lead. The opening hole at Royal Lytham & St. Annes is a par 3, and Woosnam came within inches of holing his tee shot. His birdie gave him a share of the lead.

Then disaster struck.

As he stood on the second tee, his caddie, Irishman Miles Byrne, said to him, "You're going to go ballistic. We've got two drivers in the bag."

Woosnam had been hitting two drivers on the practice tee, trying to decide which one would make the cut. Since the opening hole was a par 3, neither he nor his caddie noticed the extra driver—and the fifteenth club. The result was a two-stroke penalty. Woosnam was understandably upset and struggled through the next few holes before righting himself and finishing in a six-way tie for third place.

Without the penalty, however, he would have finished alone in second place (assuming that without the travails he wouldn't have won) and carried home an extra $312,000.

In the wake of Woosnam's mishap, a spate of similar stories surfaced. One of the most unlikely concerned Jack Nicklaus—arguably the most precise and methodical player in history.

"I was caddying for my son, Gary, in a U.S. Open qualifier," Nicklaus recalled. "We got to the 3rd hole and Gary said he wanted to hit a 4-iron. I looked in the bag and said, 'Do you want to hit your 4-iron or mine?' Before we teed off I'd counted the clubs by number—1, 2, 3, 4, etc.—but I didn't notice the extra 4-iron. Although I made the mistake as a caddie, ultimately it's the player's responsibility."

Jose Maria Olazabal has won two Masters Tournaments, but if it hadn't been for a disaster on the par-3 6th hole in 1991, he might well have won three.

The hole is arguably the easiest of the four par 3s at Augusta, and Olazabal came to the hole at five-under-par in the second round.

His tee shot wasn't great, but it wasn't all that bad either. It came up just short and to the right of the green. Given the quality of his short game, it should have led to a par or, at worst, a bogey.

Wrong.

His first pitch ran up the slope in front of the green then stopped, paused at rest for a moment, then rolled back down at his feet.

His next shot did exactly the same thing. Now he was fuming and the gallery seemed to sense what was going to happen next.

Olazabal's next shot carried to the back of the green and then, to add insult to injury, he three-putted for a record quadruple-bogey 4.

All this would have been bad enough if he hadn't gone on to rally so brilliantly.

He managed to somehow birdie four of the final seven holes and shot a one-under-par 71 for his round.

Two days later he finished the tournament in second place—one stroke behind Ian Woosnam.

As they say, golf can be a very cruel game, indeed.

BILLY FARRELL

Billy Farrell, whose father, Johnny, beat Bobby Jones in a playoff for the 1928 U.S. Open, was a fine player in his own right, for a long time one of the most successful in the metropolitan New York City area.

Billy was the head professional at The Stanwich Club in Greenwich, Connecticut, for 36 years, and in that time worked with a number of very talented amateurs. One day, a few years before he retired in 2000, one low-handicapper asked his advice about taking a shot at the Senior Tour.

"You can't beat me and I can't beat them, so why bother?" Billy reasoned with the man.

RETIEF GOOSEN

It takes luck to win any tournament, but it seems to take a little extra luck to win the U.S. Open. As two-time Open champion Cary Middlecoff once observed, "You don't win the Open. It wins you."

But some players are luckier than others. One very lucky person is South Africa's Retief Goosen, who won the 2001 Open in a playoff with Mark Brookes.

When Goosen was sixteen years old he was playing golf with his cousin, Henry Potgieter, when Goosen was hit by a bolt of lightning. The teenager was knocked unconscious. He was literally knocked out of his shoes and his clothes were burned off his body. He wasn't breathing and he was very near death.

Fortunately, there were two doctors on the course at the time. They raced to Goosen's side and administered CPR, stabilizing his condition before he was rushed to a hospital, where he spent two months recovering.

"There's no question that it changed Retief enormously," said his mother, Annetjie. "He emerged from the hospital a much humbler and quieter person."

WALTER HAGEN

Even early in his career, Walter Hagen never lacked for confidence.

When he arrived at The Country Club in Brookline, Massachusetts, in 1913 for his first U.S. Open, he casually strolled up and introduced himself to Johnny McDermott, the winner of the previous two Opens.

"Hi, you're Johnny McDermott aren't you?" he said. "I'm Walter Hagen from Rochester and I'm here to help you take care of [Harry] Vardon and [Ted] Ray."

Actually, Hagen played very well until the final round when, pressing to catch the leaders, he skied to an 80 and finished three strokes out of the next day's playoff between Vardon, Ray, and the young American amateur Francis Ouimet.

It has often been said of Walter Hagen that he made a small fortune playing golf—and spent a large fortune simply being Walter Hagen.

When figured in today's dollars, in his prime Hagen averaged $1.5 million a year, but he traveled constantly and lived lavishly, both at home and on the road.

Typical of all this was one trip to the British Open, when he required a first-class stateroom in one of the Cunard line's most luxurious liners. When he arrived in London, he commandeered the finest suite at The Savoy and had a Daimler limousine, with chauffeur and footman at his beck and call. Following the championship, he decided to do a bit of hunting and fishing, so naturally nothing would do but that he charter a plane to ferry him about the countryside.

In all, the bill for his trip came to about $90,000 in present dollars.

He couldn't have cared less.

Hagen's ascension came at a time when the Americans were beginning to wrest the domination of the sport from the British and Scottish. For this reason, and possibly because his out-of-size personality offended their sensibilities, they took a fair amount of time to warm to Hagen—although eventually they came to love him.

First, there was the matter of his decidedly unorthodox swing.

Hagen addressed the ball with an unusually wide stance, swayed to the right on the backswing, and then lurched to the left on the downswing. The good news in all this was that he generated enormous power. The bad news was that he was prone to errant shotmaking that would have been catastrophic if it weren't for his brilliant and audacious ability to recover from trouble.

When Hagen arrived at Deal for the 1920 British Open, there was much speculation in the press as to how this brash American, who had already won two U.S. Opens, might fare. Harry Vardon, the greatest player of his generation, initially refused comment on Hagen's action.

"It's decidedly unorthodox, to be sure," said England's Vardon, who had already won six British Opens. "I prefer to reserve my judgment on the chap until I can study him firsthand."

Once Vardon got a close look at Hagen, he came away unimpressed, at least by his swing.

"It is not a true swing, and therefore it is not a good swing," he sniffed.

Then there was the matter of Hagen's clothing, which was even more offensive to the British than his game.

One London paper reported that Hagen's wardrobe for the Open consisted of "a dozen golf suits, nine or ten pairs of golfing shoes, ten jerseys in a variety of different colors, almost fifty pairs of hose and any number of other items."

A writer dismissed his outfit for one round in the Open as "a scheme, or perhaps it is better described as a creation, that consisted of a black jersey without sleeves, a white shirt, white knickerbockers, and black and white shoes. All in all, it was fascinatingly esoteric."

On top of all this, Hagen refused to change in the pro shop with the rest of the professionals, and since he wasn't allowed in the clubhouse, he simply changed his shoes in his limousine, which he ordered parked in front of the clubhouse every day.

On February 28th, 1926, Walter Hagen and Bobby Jones met for a match that was variously described as either "The Battle of the Century" or the "Unofficial World Championship of Golf." Jones went off as a 3-2 favorite over Hagen, who was ten years his senior.

Jones was 3-down after the morning's play, but on the 6th hole it looked as though he might gain some ground when Hagen's drive ran into the rough and came to rest behind some trees.

After carefully (and theatrically) studying the situation, Hagen pulled out a 5-iron and tried to slice the ball around the trees. Instead, he topped the ball; but as luck would have it, the ball ran under the branches, down the fairway, through a bunker, and onto the green ten feet from the hole.

For his part, Jones hit his approach twelve feet from the hole but rimmed out his putt. Hagen nonchalantly sank his to stretch his lead to 4-up.

"I watched his shot from the rough and I thought to myself, 'Bob, you're 4-down to a man who can miss a shot like that.' When a man misses his drive, misses his second shot, and then wins the hole with a birdie, it really gets your goat."

For the record, Hagen ended the first thirty-six holes of the match 8-up on Jones.

A week later the match resumed and Hagen stretched his lead to 9-up by sinking a sixty-foot putt on the 2nd hole. He shot a 69 for the round against a 73 by Jones, and ended the third round 12-up.

By the time they reached the 7th hole in the afternoon, Hagen was 12-up with twelve holes left to play. Jones's fans found a sliver of hope when Jones chipped in for a birdie, but Hagen ended the match moments later when he chipped in as well.

For their efforts, Hagen won $6,800 and gave $5,000 to a St. Petersburg hospital. Jones received a beautiful set of cufflinks from Hagen.

While the match did provide money for charity and helped publicize the game, the United States Golf Association was not amused. They quickly prohibited amateurs from participating in any exhibitions unless all the monies were donated to charities.

While Jones, like many of his contemporaries, could find playing with Hagen an exasperating experience, he greatly admired the man's abilities and his approach to the game.

"Many of the fellows find it difficult to play with Walter but I love it," Jones said. "He walks along with his chin up, smiling away, and never complains about the bad breaks. He just plays the ball as he finds it, and heavens knows he comes closer to beating luck itself than anyone I know."

Today, players have swing coaches and sports psychologists to help them navigate the murky waters of the game at the highest levels. This would have struck Walter Hagen as absurd. In fact, his approach to the game was brilliant in its simplicity and well-worth copying for pros and hackers alike.

"If I hit one into the rough, I always try to tell myself that I'll get a good lie and will be able to get the ball out safely," he told a writer. "Either way, I always tell myself that my job is to post a good score and do the best I can. I know I'm going to miss a few shots during a round. Everyone does, no matter how good they are, so when I miss one, I'm set for it. I just write it off and say that was one of the ones I was due to miss. If you worry about the ones you miss, you'll just keep on missing them."

BEN HOGAN

Ben Hogan's victory in the 1953 British Open at Carnoustie was one of the most memorable in the history of the championship. Initially reluctant to make the trip to Scotland, he was finally talked into entering the championship by Gene Sarazen and Walter Hagen.

If there was ever a man made for a course, Hogan was the man for Carnoustie, perhaps the most demanding course on the Open rota and certainly one of the sternest tests in golf.

The Scots revered Hogan and his tough, no-nonsense approach to the game. That reverence only increased as the championship played itself out. Even today, they regard his victory in his only appearance in the Open as the stuff of legend—no more so than for the way he played the brutal par-5 6th hole, named "Long."

The greatest challenge is from the tee, where the best approach for a second shot requires players to drive down the left side of the hole, which is guarded on the left by an out-of-bounds fence and on the right by a bunker in the center of the fairway. Between the rough and the bunker is a mere twenty yards of fairway.

In each round, Hogan started the ball out along to the out-of-bounds line and then cut it back safely into the fairway.

How difficult is this shot? Even lacking the pressure of the British Open, it is so difficult that when the late Payne Stewart came to Carnoustie in 1991, he was asked if he planned to follow Hogan's example when he came to the 6th hole.

"No," Stewart said. "I'm not that good."

For as long as there have been great golfers, people have pondered what it is that drives people to become champions—to take that step beyond the very good into the rarified air of greatness.

Ben Hogan was never a person who was prone to deep introspection, at least for public consumption. But something he said late in life sheds light on what it was that made Hogan one of the game's greatest champions.

"I'm sure I get more satisfaction out of hitting golf shots than anyone who ever lived," he said. "Sure, I liked to win, but more than anything else, I took tremendous pleasure out of playing the game the way I thought it should be played, and that meant hitting the shot that was called for. If I did it under the pressure of competition and it allowed me to win, so much the better, but what I really loved was seeing the shot and then hitting it properly. That's golf to me."

In the latter years of his life, Hogan would go to Shady Oaks and hit practice balls at an isolated part of the course. But inevitably, as he grew older, even that became too much for him. Still, he never lost his love for, or fascination with, the game.

"Ben enjoyed his last years, but he very much missed hitting balls and trying to figure it all out," remembered his wife of sixty-two years, Valerie. "He kept his hand in his club company, but nothing ever replaced the satisfaction he got from just hitting that golf ball. Finally, practicing just became too painful for Ben, but he'd still like to swing a club around the house. My sister did think there was a certain sadness to Ben when he could no longer do what he wanted to do—which was hit balls. The accident cheated Ben out of years of golf, but he was never bitter about it. He was quietly religious. He never wore his faith on his sleeve. That wasn't his way. But we were always thankful that he survived the accident and God let him live. We realized how fortunate we were that he got to play again, but as he got older there was a sense of loss. More than anything else, Ben wished he could have played forever."

"People today don't fully appreciate the magnificent accuracy of Ben's ball-striking," recalls two-time PGA Champion Paul Runyan. "There's a story that I've heard from more than one player about a time when Ben was practicing 3-irons and he hit his caddie on the head, knocking him down. They claim that Ben hit him two more times before the caddie got back on his feet. I don't think the story is true, not because Ben was incapable of such accuracy—because he most certainly was—but because it wouldn't have been enough of a challenge for him."

Ben Hogan and Arnold Palmer were never particularly close. Part of this was due to their personalities.

"Ben was a very shy man who went about playing in a very businesslike manner," recalls five-time British Open Champion Peter Thomson. "Arnold very much liked strutting the stage. He was very much a showman."

Also, their games couldn't have been more different. Hogan was very controlled and precise, where Palmer was the ultimate scrambler.

And so when Hogan was named as captain of the 1967 Ryder Cup team, many people speculated that there could be fireworks between the team's captain and its biggest star.

Hogan referred to Palmer as "fella" throughout the week, never once referring to him as "Arnold" or "Arnie."

Hogan paired Palmer with Gardner Dickinson—one of Hogan's closest friends—on Friday, and they won both of their matches, which lifted Palmer's Ryder Cup record to 11-3-2.

Following the day's play, Palmer took one of the British players for a flight in his plane. This reportedly infuriated Hogan, and when the next day's Fourball pairing was announced, Palmer's name was missing from the list.

"Did Arnold ask to sit out Saturday morning's match?" a writer asked Hogan.

"No," Hogan said.

"Why isn't he playing then?" the writer persisted.

"Because I'm the captain and I decide who plays and who doesn't," said Hogan.

"Then why won't he be playing?" asked the writer.

"Because I say he won't," Hogan replied.

"Is there a reason?" another writer asked.

"Yes," said Hogan.

"May I ask what the reason is?" a third writer asked.

"Yes, you can ask, but I won't tell you," Hogan said.

In the 1980s, Ben Hogan shot a series of television commercials for his equipment company. The shooting took place at the Riviera Country Club, where Hogan won a U.S. Open and two Los Angeles Opens.

The director and crew arrived well ahead of Hogan and set up their equipment. As the time approached for Hogan to arrive, the director told the crew that Hogan was a perfectionist and they should expect the shoot to last at least two hours.

When Hogan arrived, he asked the director what he was supposed to do.

"Just hit the ball onto the green, Mr. Hogan," the director said.

"What do you want it to do when it lands on the green?" Hogan asked.

"What do you mean, Mr. Hogan?" the director asked.

"Do you want it to spin back, spin left, or spin right?" Hogan asked.

"It would be great if you could make it spin left, Mr. Hogan," the man said.

Once everyone was ready, Hogan hit his shot. The ball landed on the green, jumped forward, and then kicked to the left, ending up two inches from the hole.

"How was that?" Hogan asked the director.

"Fine, Mr. Hogan," the director said.

For all intents and purposes, the shoot was over.

Today, any number of Tour pros are involved in golf course architecture, but Ben Hogan only designed one course in his life, The Trophy Club, in Dallas.

Plans called for two courses, one a true championship test designed to attract a Tour event to Dallas, the second a more member-friendly layout. But financial problems beset the project and only eighteen holes were designed by Hogan and architect Joe Lee.

The problems began when the original developer was forced out and Hogan almost immediately found himself at odds with the people who were funding the project. Hogan had developed plans for a beautiful clubhouse where he would keep his trophies and awards on display. He also planned to build a house on the property. When the financiers told him that he would have to find five hundred more members before a clubhouse would be built, Hogan walked.

Still, the holes that were built reflected much of what Hogan believed a golf course should be.

First of all, there should be no blind shots.

"I don't like blind shots," Hogan said. "I never could play by radar."

Next, the course should be a fair test but not ridiculously difficult.

"I don't understand people who build golf courses you can't shoot a good score on," Hogan said. "If they want to do that, why don't they just dump rocks all over them?"

Not surprisingly, Hogan was involved in every aspect of the design. He walked the property, climbing over fences so often that his legs, which were badly damaged in a 1949 automobile accident, ached and throbbed and were swollen by the end of the day. He personally marked every single tree he wanted removed. He ensured the routing was balanced between dogleg lefts and dogleg rights. He even hits shots to make sure the shot values required were proper.

"One day he was out there in khaki pants and work boots and he hit a 4-wood almost 200 yards to the green from a bare lie," remembers Joe Lee. "The ball split the green. I couldn't believe it, even from Ben Hogan."

So how good is the course?

The best answer might be the description offered by Hogan's old friend and rival, Byron Nelson, who played the course just after its 1976 opening.

"It's pretty much like you'd expect a course designed by Ben to be," Nelson said. "It's long and hard."

Ben Hogan was a reserved, almost shy man, who was often misunderstood and even enigmatic to most people, even some who had known him for much of his life. The public, for example, would have been surprised to learn of his great affection for two dogs that lived at Shady Oaks, his country club in Fort Worth.

Max was an Australian shepherd and Buster was a little Schnauzer. When Hogan drove around the course in a cart, the dogs would run along beside the cart or ride on the passenger's seat. When Hogan went into the clubhouse for lunch, the dogs would sit under the window where he sat, and invariably, he would ask one of the staff to make sure the dogs got something to eat.

When Buster died, the club decided to bury him in a spot between the pro shop and the putting green. On the day the dog was buried, Hogan came to the club dressed in a dark suit. He went to the gravesite, took off his hat and put it over his heart, and then he put his fingers to his lips, kissed them, and held them to the gravestone for a moment, saying good-bye.

One time a friend, knowing the Hogans' love of dogs, gave them a toy poodle and suggested they name him "Champ."

"We can't do that," Hogan told his wife, Valerie. "People will think I'm thinking about myself."

"Well, Ben, what do you think we should name him?" Valerie asked.

"How about 'Duffer'?" Hogan suggested.

The name stuck.

The late Dave Marr, who won the 1965 PGA Championship and went on to be a much-acclaimed golf analyst for both ABC and NBC, had a theory that for many top golfers, there's one loss—one setback—that they never quite recover from. He pointed to Arnold Palmer's loss to Billy Casper in the 1966 U.S. Open at the Olympic Club, Tom Weiskopf's loss to Jack Nicklaus in the 1975 Masters, and most poignantly, Ben Hogan's loss to Dr. Cary Middlecoff in the 1956 U.S. Open at Oak Hill, when he missed a three-foot putt on the 71st hole to lose by a stroke.

But there would be one more close call in the Open for Hogan, and that came in 1960, when he dueled with Arnold Palmer and a twenty-year-old amateur named Jack Nicklaus on the final day.

Almost unbelievably, Hogan came to the par-5 17th having hit every green in regulation. Tied for the lead, he hit a fine drive, then laid up short of the green with a 4-iron. His ball came to rest about fifty yards short of the water that protected the front of the green.

The pin was cut on the very front of the green, a mere fifteen feet away from the water. Hogan studied the shot with his customary intensity, and then he pulled a wedge from his bag.

"I was putting just horribly, and knew that I had to get it very close to have any chance of making it," Hogan recalled. "I had the most beautiful lie you've ever seen. I couldn't have placed the ball in a better lie. I wanted to put as much stuff on the ball as I possibly could, so I could keep it below the hole. I hit what I thought was a perfect shot. I hit it just the way I wanted, and actually felt my spine tingle as I watched it leave the club. But I just misjudged the shot."

The ball hit the green, but spun back into the water, and Hogan had to settle for a bogey. Desperately gambling on the 18th, he hit his drive into the water and had to take a triple bogey.

"It was just the saddest thing you've ever seen," said his wife, Valerie, years later. "If he had only won it would have been such a wonderful ending."

When Ben Hogan traveled to Carnoustie for the 1953 British Open, the locals were in awe of the player they called "The Wee Ice Mon." The Scots are a notoriously difficult people to impress, particularly when it comes to golf, but Hogan managed the trick nicely.

One day he greatly impressed a group of spectators who were watching him hit practice balls—particularly when he hit twenty perfect two-woods from the turf without regripping the club even once.

When he was playing the Tour, Ben Hogan's best friend was Jimmy Demaret, although the two men could not have been more different.

Hogan was shy and reserved. Demaret was colorful and flamboyant. Hogan practiced relentlessly. Demaret saw him hitting balls one day after a tournament round and wandered over to ask what he was doing.

Their differences were neatly summed up in this dispatch from British writer Henry Longhurst during the 1951 Ryder Cup matches from Pinehurst #2. After days of blisteringly hot weather, the opening day of the Matches dawned brutally cold.

"Among the gallery in the fourth match of the day, bearing no outward or visible sign connecting him with the proceedings, is a small dark man with gray raincoat, gray cap, gray trousers and inscrutable expression, looking somewhat like a Pinkerton guard on unobtrusive watch for pickpock-

ets. This is the world's greatest golfer, Ben Hogan, participating in the Ryder Cup Matches. His partner, the normally
flamboyant Jimmy Demaret, is concealed in a flowing check
Ulster with a distinctly Sherlock Holmes air. From time to
time, they step forward, remove their heavy clothing, give the
ball a resounding slam, and return to anonymity."

THE IRISH

A group of golfers from Ballybunion traveled to the United States for a tour of some of the famous courses along the eastern seaboard. As luck would have it, one of their first stops was Winged Foot Golf Club in the New York City suburb of Mamaroneck. This was fortunate for two reasons: First, the two courses at Winged Foot are among the best in the world. Second, the membership at Winged Foot tilts heavily toward the area's Irish-American community, so the visitors were certain to be welcomed by kindred spirits only a few generations removed from the loving embrace of Mother Ireland herself.

Their arrival coincided with an unusual period of cold, early fall weather, and following their morning round, the group and their hosts stopped for lunch in the grillroom. A round of drinks was served, and as they awaited the arrival of lunch, one of the Winged Foot members asked his guest if he'd like another drink, just to fortify himself for the afternoon's play.

"I'll have another whisky, if you'd be so kind," the Ballybunion member said.

"Would you like a drop of water in it?" the Winged Foot member asked.

"Only if there's room," the Irishman replied.

On the same visit, one of the Winged Foot members ordered a "Rusty Nail," which is a lovely drink made up of equal parts scotch whisky and Drambuie, a liquor made in Scotland.

"Aye, that's what we call a 'Putting Mixture' back home," his Irish guest said.

"Why's that?" the American asked.

"Because one of those and it's certain there'll be a great deal of mixed putting to follow," the Irishman replied, no doubt knowingly.

Ballybunion Golf Club is one of the favorite stops for American golfers visiting Ireland. One group of golfers happened to drop by during a particularly rainy stretch.

"Does it often rain like this?" the American asked his caddie.

"Not at all," said the caddie. "In fact, last year it just rained twice—once for six months and the other for three. Aside from those downpours, the weather was glorious."

Ireland's Joe Carr was one of the world's greatest amateurs in the 1950s and '60s, winning every important amateur event in Ireland and the British Isles, and participated in several Walker Cup matches as both a player and captain. In addition, he was the first Irishman to serve as captain of the Royal & Ancient Golf Club of St. Andrews.

One year he was asked to referee a match at Pebble Beach. He was introduced as "Mr. J. B. Carr, of Dublin, England, Captain of the Royal and Ancient Golf Club of St. Andrews in Scotland."

"Wars have been started for less than that," Carr whispered to a friend.

TONY JACKLIN

Tony Jacklin's victory in the 1969 British Open at Royal Lytham & St. Annes was enormously popular since it was the first victory for an Englishman since Max Faulkner won in 1951.

With the weight of the championship—not to mention his countrymen's hopes—weighing on him, he decided he'd best take a sleeping pill and try to get a good night's rest.

It took a while for the pill to kick in, so he decided to watch a late movie on television. Sure enough, he fell asleep. In fact, it was so deep a sleep that Bert Yancey, who was sharing a house with the Jacklins, couldn't wake him. So Yancey did the only logical thing: he picked up Jacklin, carried him upstairs, and laid him down on his bed.

Give the late Bert Yancey an assist.

BOBBY JONES

Bobby Jones was the ultimate gentleman and sportsman, but even as a youngster, he was a fierce competitor.

The fourteen-year-old Jones arrived at Merion for the 1916 U.S. Amateur, his first attempt at the championship. Everything went along smoothly until the second round, when he faced Frank Dyer, the Pennsylvania amateur champion.

Jones trailed in the match but pulled even on the 16th hole and took the lead by winning the 17th. On the 18th hole, both players drove into the rough. Both were playing Spalding "Red Honor" balls. One ball was in a good lie while the other had settled down into the deep rough. The players argued, for a time vehemently, about which ball belonged to which player. Finally, Jones agreed to play from the poor lie, and it cost him the hole.

The two stopped for lunch, but Jones wasn't taking any chances in the afternoon round.

"I've put so many Js on these balls that he can't help but see them," he told a friend.

Jones came out, won the 1st hole, and never looked back. He closed Dyer out, 4 & 2, but lost to the defending champion, Robert Gardner, in the next round.

Following his graduation from Georgia Tech, Bob Jones traveled north to Cambridge, where he studied English Literature at Harvard. While he didn't play on the golf team because he had used up his eligibility while at Georgia Tech, he served as the team's manager. He did, however, play practice rounds with the team and occasionally played in exhibitions to raise funds for the team and the school. The other crucial element of his job was keeping track of the team's whisky supply—a responsibility that he happily accepted with great fervor.

One day, on a lark, he played the six-man team's best ball—and won.

Bob Jones played in the first few Masters, even though his competitive career ended in 1930 with his victories in the U.S. and British Opens and Amateurs—the historic Grand Slam.

Still, he was an enormous favorite of the galleries, as writer Herbert Warren Wind learned.

Wind was walking down the right side of the 10th fairway with a friend and commenting on a particular player's swing, saying he thought it was the finest and most beautiful swing in the game. A man standing nearby overheard him and begged to differ.

"Sir, Bobby's still playing," he said.

BERNHARD LANGER

Germany's Bernhard Langer, a two-time Masters champion, is a notoriously deliberate player.

At one point in his career, he sported a beard.

"See that man there?" Lee Trevino quipped. "When he started his round today he was clean shaven."

During the 2001 British Open at Royal Lytham & St. Annes, ABC golf commentator Peter Alliss watched as Langer meticulously studied a shot.

"I venture that one of the smallest books in the world would be *Shots I Played in Haste*, by Bernhard Langer."

JACK LEMMON

Jack Lemmon, the brilliant actor who died in 2001 at age seventy-six, was a passionate golfer, who played in twenty-five AT&T Pebble Beach National Pro-Ams. He loved the tournament so much that he would have his film projects scheduled around the event.

"Jack was a golf nut," recalled Eric Monte, the professional emeritus at Lemmon's home course, Hillcrest, in Los Angeles. "He always practiced a lot, especially in the weeks before the Crosby. He always looked forward to playing with Peter Jacobsen (his partner for fifteen years). He was very diligent about his game."

Indeed, one of the tournament's enduring themes over the last decade or so of his life was Lemmon's quixotic quest to score well enough to play on Sunday.

In Jacobsen, he had the perfect partner. In 1999, they came to a par 3 and Lemmon worried over his club selection.

"What are you hitting?" he asked Jacobsen.

"A 5-iron," Jacobsen said.

"I better hit a 4 then," Lemmon said.

"Jack," said Jacobsen, "4-iron, 9-iron, 4-wood, at your age it doesn't matter. They all go the same distance anyway."

In 1991, Lemmon arrived at the tournament and announced that this, after all the years of frustration, was certain to be the year he'd make the cut and play on Sunday.

"I've got a herniated disc, a pulled muscle in my right leg, and the worst case of sciatica in medical history," he said. "I'm a lock."

For much of the tournament's history, the magnificent Cypress Point Club was part of the three-course rotation. Of all the wonderful holes at Cypress Point, none is more terrifying than the par-3 16th, which requires a carry of more than two hundred yards over an inlet. The hole is made even more frightening by the sound of waves crashing against the rocks and the winds that gust off the ocean.

What is a hole like this to a man like Jack Lemmon?

One year he arrived at the hole and walked to the very edge of the cliff like a smaller version of John Wayne and stared intently at the waters pounding on the rocks.

Then he bent over, picked a few blades of grass, and tossed them into the air to judge the strength of the wind.

The grass blew back into his face in a scene worthy of his epic comedy, *Mister Roberts*.

Undeterred, Lemmon strode dramatically back to the tee, pulled his club, addressed the ball—and hit it into the Pacific.

The team of Lemmon and Jacobsen (it actually sounds like an old vaudeville act, come to think of it) had their last best chance of playing on Sunday in 1991.

They began Saturday's round with only an outside chance of making the cut, but as the day went on, they rallied and the guys at CBS, who were televising the tournament, reveled in their performance. They were the stars of the show that day.

On the 6th hole, Lemmon hooked his drive past the gallery ropes. When he reached his ball, it had nestled down in the rough.

He took a practice swing.

"Poetry," he announced to the gallery, and then he somehow managed to come up with a swing that not only got the ball out of the rough but well down the fairway. It was close enough that he could save par, which meant a net birdie for the team.

He made a couple of pars on the way in and then they came to 18, where Lemmon—under the weight of finally making the cut after all those years—outdrove his son, Chris.

The projected cut was 15-under-par. They were 14 under. The gallery was going berserk. The CBS guys were going berserk. And when Jacobsen sank his twenty-footer for birdie, the place erupted.

Jacobsen threw his visor into a nearby bunker. He and Lemmon hugged. All was right with the world.

Alas, golf is a cruel game.

The cut came in at 13-under-par. However, Lemmon was undeterred.

"All in all, this is the best week I've ever had here," he said. "Boy, did we have a day. And if I don't make it this year, well, then there's next year."

BRUCE LIETZKE

After finishing his college career at the University of Houston, Bruce Lietzke struggled with his game and soon lost interest. His father suggested he get a job in the real world to see if it might renew his interest in the game.

"I went to work as a security guard working the night shift," Lietzke recalls. "They gave me a gun and one bullet and then they locked the bullet in the desk drawer. It's a good thing no one ever came and tried to rob the place."

NANCY LOPEZ

In 1978, Nancy Lopez captured the nation's attention by winning five tournaments in a row. It was just the shot of publicity the LPGA needed to truly put it on the sporting map of the country.

Her fifth victory came in the Bankers Trust Classic in Rochester, New York, but something that happened in the first round almost sent her packing.

On the 10th hole, her drive flew into the gallery and hit one of the spectators, a Dr. Jerry Mesolla, on the head. By the time Lopez reached him, there was blood pouring from a cut on his forehead. In tears, Lopez took his hand and asked if he was all right.

"Fine," he said. "I'm glad I finally got a chance to meet you."

GARY MCCORD

Gary McCord, the irreverent CBS golf announcer and player on the Senior Tour, was paired with Jack Nicklaus in the 2000 MasterCard Championship, the season-opening event on the Senior Tour.

Playing the Hualalai Golf Club, McCord shanked a 2-iron tee shot to the par-3 5th hole. The ball came to rest in the jagged lava and McCord looked on in horror as Nicklaus climbed onto the rocks to look for McCord's ball.

"I've got sixty-year-old Jack Nicklaus, new hip and all, climbing around on the rocks looking for a ball I shanked there," said McCord. "I was sure he was going to fall and break his hip. That would add to the legacy of my mediocre career. Kicked out of the Masters. Ended the career of the greatest golfer who ever played the game."

MERION GOLF CLUB

The Merion Golf Club in the "Main Line" Philadelphia suburb of Ardmore is one of the most historic and splendid places in all of golf. It has hosted sixteen national championships including the 1930 U.S. Amateur, where Bobby Jones completed his Grand Slam, and the 1950 U.S. Open, won by Ben Hogan following his near-fatal automobile accident.

Merion's East course is sublime and the old, well-worn clubhouse is everything a clubhouse should be, as well as being a repository of much golf history and memorabilia.

Like many old, traditional clubs, Merion is occasionally slow to adapt to change, especially when it feels pushed by the outside world. But when it finally elected a woman to the Board of Governors, it picked the perfect one: Pam Emory.

Pam was a splendid golfer, a longtime member of the USGA's Women's Committee, as well as its Museum and Library Committee and the Girls' Junior Committee. She was also a gentle and insightful writer (an occupation they didn't hold against her), and a person whose love for the game and its people was deep and abiding.

Sadly, she was stricken with cancer and put up a long and brave fight against the disease. In the months before her death in September 2000 at age fifty-one, she visited with a fellow writer and longtime friend. Her spirits were good, even jovial, and she was hoping for some writing assignments to help cover the cost of the yellow Porsche she had purchased in an exquisite act of defiance toward the cancer.

The chemotherapy and other treatments had dramatically altered her appearance. Her once thick, red hair had been reduced to just some thin strands along the sides and back of her head, leaving her virtually bald on the top. This, combined with wire-rimmed glasses and a pink, almost elfin glow to her face, struck her as both funny and ironic.

"It took cancer, but after all these years, I finally look like a member of the board at Merion," she joked.

JOHNNY MILLER

Johnny Miller's work as a golf analyst for NBC Sports has earned him widespread praise, in large part because of his insights and his candor.

One case in point came during a tournament where Jack Nicklaus, admittedly past his prime, was challenging for the lead in difficult, windy conditions.

"I talked to Jack last night and asked him what adjustments he makes when he's playing in the wind," Miller said. "He said, 'It's easy John. I just move the club one groove up on the ball.' Now folks, I think you know that I'm a pretty good golfer and I have to tell you that I have no idea what the man is talking about."

MOTHER ENGLAND

People can debate all they'd like about the origins of the game, and certainly there are cases to be made that it got its start on the frozen rivers of Holland or even in Japan, given certain old illustrations.

That notwithstanding, there's no argument that the game's roots are firmly planted in Scotland and throughout the British Isles and the countries that made up the British Empire at one time or another. Just as surely as the sun never set on Queen Victoria's Empire, it also never set on the game of golf once the British took it to the far corners of the globe.

Happily, the British and their home cousins produced an astonishing wealth of characters and, therefore, stories to report.

At Prestwick Golf Club, the site of the first twelve British Opens beginning in 1860, one of the most formidable members was one Major Neilson. One day he was seated alone in the most sanctified part of the clubhouse, the Smoke Room, reading his newspaper, when he was approached by a young man named Morty Dykes.

"Isn't it a beautiful morning, sir?" said Dykes, who would go on to win the Scottish Amateur Championship.

Without bothering to either look up from the news of the day or acknowledge the existence of Mr. Morty Dykes, the Major reached up and pressed the bell over his chair. In a matter of mere moments, an attendant appeared.

"Steward," the Major said, pausing only to turn the page. "There seems to be a young man here who wishes to discuss the weather. Would you be so good as to accommodate him?"

Major Neilson was no less charitable in his relations with established members. One day a longtime member, Dr. Percy Walker, was summoned by Prestwick's club secretary (a very powerful position in British golf clubs) and asked to attend to the Major, who had fallen in the men's room. Dr. Walker raced to the men's lavatory, only to find the elderly Major Neilson flat on his back.

"I immediately kneeled over to take the Major's pulse," said Dr. Walker. "As I did, the Major opened his eyes, riveted me with his gaze, and said, 'Unhand me, sir, and go away. If I require medical assistance I shall rise and summon my own practitioner.'"

Dr. Walker had another run-in with a formidable member who also happened to be a veteran of the British army, one Major Galloway.

It seems that one night at a Prestwick club dinner in the 1950s, the club secretary summoned Dr. Walker from an adjoining table to treat Major Galloway, who had somehow managed to slide under the table.

Once again, Dr. Walker raced to the rescue, scrambling under the table, where he encountered the prostrate major. After a moment's examination, he came back from under the table where an anxious room filled with fellow members awaited the medical update.

"Is the major all right?" the Captain inquired.

"Quite, just a bit drunk," the doctor reported.

"And you, sir, are fired," roared the Major from under the table.

Royal St. Georges Golf Club in Sandwich first hosted the British Open in 1894, the first time it had been played outside of Scotland, and has hosted it several times since, most recently in 1993 when Greg Norman won the Old Claret Jug for the second time.

The club has enormous panache and elegance, and has been the home club for many of Great Britain and Ireland's most celebrated amateurs, including Laddie Lucas, Michael Bonallack, and Gerald Micklem. For these, and a variety of other reasons, there's a certain snob appeal attached to membership at Royal St. Georges.

Some years ago, a prospective member was asked why he wished to leave his present club—which was less than an hour's drive from Royal St. Georges.

"Well, St. Georges is closer to my home," he replied. "My present club demands too great a commute."

"And where is your home?" he was asked.

"Chile," he said.

Some Americans visiting one of the old English clubs finished their round and asked where they might take a shower.

"I'm terribly sorry, but we don't have showers here," they were told. "Our members bathe at home."

Even though we are into the twenty-first century, many golf clubs in the British Isles still regard women the way they regard a turf disease: something that clearly exists but must be watched with a careful eye at all times. To say that change comes at a glacial pace at many clubs is to say that the Titantic was a very big ship that had a small run-in with an iceberg. In other words, it's a colossal understatement.

One day a member and his wife stood on the first tee at one of the stuffier clubs, when a fellow member approached.

"I see you're alone," he said to his fellow member, totally ignoring the lady in question. "Mind if I join you?"

Some American tourists were taking a golf vacation through Great Britain. They played St. Andrews and Royal Lytham & St. Annes and then traveled to Wales for a round at Royal St. David's in Harlech.

On the day they were supposed to play, a storm came crashing in off the water. The rain was coming down in sheets and the wind was whipping so hard that from the club-house they could see the flagstick on the 18th green was blown so far sideways that the flag came close to touching the putting surface.

One of the Americans struck up a conversation with the club's professional and the subject turned to the difficulty of the course.

"Oh, 'tis fine on a day like today, but if the wind is blowing it can be a real bugger," the pro said with a perfectly straight face.

While there have been enormous advances in course maintenance over the years, at many clubs in the British Isles, the greens keeper is considered a part of the club family. The job is often a lifelong position.

At one club, the greens keeper had worked there almost his entire adult life. When the time came for him to retire and his last day finally came around, he decided to take one last walk around the course he had loved and tended to over the years. Less than an hour later, he returned to the club-house and ran into one of the old members.

"I stopped after six holes," he said. "I couldn't go on. I love the old girl too much."

Bob Parker is the longtime professional at Swinley Forest Golf Club, which has more than its share of rather eccentric, older members. He fondly recalls one who was particularly frugal.

"This fellow came in and wanted to purchase a pair of socks, but he insisted on trying them out first," Parker recalled. "He wore them for two rounds and then purchased them. Fourteen years later he came into the shop and said, 'I say, Parker, I must get some more of those wonderful socks from you. I think the previous pair has about worn out.'"

Traditionally, a large part of the membership at Royal St. Georges has been comprised of men who had attended Eton, the exclusive public school (called a private school in the United States). Old School Ties—in a manner of speaking—run deep among Etonians, and nowhere is that more the case than at Royal St. Georges.

One day a member of an old, middle European, aristocratic family came to Royal St. Georges to play a high-stakes match against an American of considerable wealth, if not necessarily breeding.

When they arrived on the first tee, they were told by the starter that they would have to wait in deference to a group of old Etonians who had gathered for their regular match.

After waiting for what seemed like an eternity while the old boys arranged matches and teed off, the European finally became exasperated.

"Can't we please go ahead and play?" he asked the starter. "Who cares about these old fools from Estonia?"

Brigadier Rupert Scot was the club secretary at Rye Golf Club from 1948 until 1961, and to say he was authoritarian is to put it mildly. In fact, the man could be positively frightening.

Not only was the Brigadier physically imposing, with his military bearing, but those who visited his home couldn't help but notice the human skull that rested on the mantel.

It seems that during World War II, the Brigadier served in the British Army in the Pacific. One day a Japanese sniper killed two of his men, and the Brigadier tracked him down, killed him, then beheaded him and brought the skull back to England at the close of the war.

Not surprisingly, the Brigadier was something of a stickler about the club's rules and occasionally resorted to extreme measures to see they were enforced.

Early one evening he happened to gaze out his office window and saw two members having a putting contest on the 18th green. He went to his desk, pulled his old service revolver from a drawer, and fired off one round, hitting a ball on the green.

The players turned in shock to see the Brigadier framed in the window, laughing loudly.

Change comes slowly to England's golf clubs, which is just the way the members like it. At one club, a man was repeatedly offered the presidency and was steadfast in his refusal to be burdened with the office. Finally, he relented, with one condition.

"I will accept, only if I don't have to do anything," he said

"Oh, quite," he was told. "That's the idea."

The Honourable Company of Edinburgh is a notoriously conservative, all-male club in Muirfield, Scotland. To say they are resistant to change or any altering of tradition is an enormous understatement.

But when Barbara Nicklaus visited the club several years ago at least one tradition went by the boards. Not only did they invite her into the clubhouse, they even gave her a tour.

To everyone's amazement, the world didn't come to an end.

An American visitor was having a bit of lunch after his round at one of England's starchier clubs when one of the members asked him about his club in the States.

"We've changed a lot over the years," the American explained. "We actually have quite a diverse cross-section of members now."

"Oh, dear," the Englishman said. "We haven't that problem here."

The British have benefited over the centuries from being an island nation. This has kept pesky sorts like the French and Germans at bay during certain periods of nastiness brought on by overreaching continentals like Napoleon and Hitler, just to name two.

Of course, this has made the British somewhat insular as regards the world away from their shores, the Empire notwithstanding. This is part of their collective charm. Take, for example the newspaper headline "HEAVY FOG CUTS OFF EUROPE FROM BRITAIN."

Then there was this reaction to Walter Hagen's speech following his victory in the 1922 British Open—the first by a player born in America.

"It was a very modest speech," said J. H. Taylor, the winner of five British Opens. "It was a tribute to British sportsmanship."

An American named Warren (Bud) Gilbert Jr., a three-time winner of the Jasper (Alberta, Canada) Invitational, was planning a trip to Scotland and hoped to play Muirfield. He had the secretary of his club, the Capilano Country Club in Vancouver, British Columbia, write a letter of introduction and arrange for a day's play.

When Mr. Gilbert arrived, he was greeted warmly and paired with a fellow American. In the course of the round, his playing partner told him how difficult he had found it for an American to be accepted by the members, who apparently didn't quite share in the much-celebrated "Special Relationship" celebrated by politicians on either side of the Atlantic.

When Mr. Gilbert told him that the letter of introduction had been arranged through his club in Vancouver, a light went on in his partner's head.

"No wonder," he said. "They think you're a Canadian."

THE NATIONAL GOLF LINKS

Membership in The National Golf Links, on the eastern end of Long Island, is something much prized, not only for the quality of the golf course, but for the atmosphere that envelops the club.

So it shouldn't have come as a surprise that one prospective member was delighted when he learned that his sponsor had arranged for him to play in a club tournament where, by the luck of the draw, he would face the club's powerful president.

Now you would think that, given such an opportunity, a prospective member would, if not tank the match, at least be on his best behavior. Alas, that wasn't the case. Apparently, the man's competitive instincts got the better of his common sense. When the club's president missed a putt for a halve, the man said a much-too-audible "Yes!"

"No," said the club's president, succinctly summing up the man's chances of joining The National Golf Links.

JACK NICKLAUS

Jack Nicklaus excelled in a variety of sports as a youngster, basketball and football among them. But it was clear from an early age that golf was his passion. By the time he was twelve he broke 80 for the first time, shooting a 74 at Scioto Country Club, the site of Bobby Jones's victory in the 1926 U.S. Open.

The next year, young Jack set a goal of breaking 70, and one afternoon while playing golf with his father, Charlie, he shot a two-under-par 34 on the front nine. Naturally, he was anxious to tee it up on the back, but his father insisted that they go home for dinner first.

In what was probably one of the fastest dinners in the history of the Nicklaus family, father and son sped through their meal and returned to Scioto where, by the end of 17 holes, he was one-under-par and in need of an eagle on the 500-yard, par-5 18th for his 69.

By now, darkness was settling over the course and the sprinklers were turned on. Hardly ideal conditions, but Nicklaus pounded a good drive and stung a 2-iron thirty-five feet from the hole. With the sprinklers click-clacking and barely able to see the hole, much less read the water-soaked green, Nicklaus ran in the eagle putt for the first of his hundreds of rounds in the 60s.

Jack Nicklaus shot a 51 the first time he played nine holes of golf. He shot a 61 the second time and a 71 the third time.

"It was my first experience with choking," he joked.

Certainly, no player knows more about winning than Jack Nicklaus does; but he also understands how painful a loss can be.

In the 1989 PGA Championship at Kemper Lakes, he watched Mike Reid blow a three-stroke lead on the final three holes to lose to Payne Stewart. When Reid, a quiet, unassuming player, finished his round, he sat dejectedly in the locker room. Nicklaus approached him and asked if they could talk.

"Mike, I just want to tell you that I've never felt so badly for anyone in my entire life. You played too well not to win. I'm sorry."

Reid was understandably moved.

"For Jack, the greatest player in history, to say that to me was very humbling," Reid said. "It added so much humanness to things. I just thought, 'you know, this is terrible, but life goes on.' And it does."

Jack Nicklaus was having lunch during the 2000 PGA Seniors' Championship when he was interrupted by a man's persistent banging on a nearby window. Finally, Nicklaus went to the window to see what the man wanted.

"Hey, is Arnie in there?" the man asked.

"Sorry, he's not," said Nicklaus.

"Okay, thanks, pal," the man said.

Jack Nicklaus was playing Pebble Beach one day when a wave of fog rolled in, reducing visibility to less than one hundred yards. When he was told that play was going to be postponed, Nicklaus was mystified.

"I haven't been able to see that far in years," he quipped.

In fact, in 1986 when he won his sixth Masters, he almost made a hole in one on the 16th hole.

"When he hit his drive, the ball had barely left the club-face and I said 'Be close' and he said, 'It is,'" his son Jackie, who was caddying for him, recalled. "The amazing thing is he probably hadn't actually seen a ball land on that green in ten years."

On the face of things, Jack Nicklaus and Lee Trevino would seem to be unlikely friends.

Nicklaus grew up in relative affluence in Columbus, Ohio. Trevino grew up in grinding poverty in Dallas.

Nicklaus's best friend was his father, Charlie. Trevino never knew his father.

Nicklaus learned the game from one of its most respected teachers, Jack Grout. Trevino dug it out of the dirt—literally—on his own.

Nicklaus honed his game playing in the major amateur events, winning the U.S. Amateur twice. Trevino learned the game by betting over his head in matches at Dallas's notorious Tennison Park.

But at the height of their respective games, no one ever offered Nicklaus a sterner or a more sustained challenge than Trevino. Indeed, only Tom Watson equaled Trevino's challenge.

The only Major championship to elude Trevino was the Masters. People have speculated that he never felt comfortable at Augusta National, and that may be at least partially true. But a more important reason is that he realized the golf course never really suited his game and he was smart enough not to alter it for one week a year.

"I'm a 'mudder,'" Trevino once explained. "There's only two ways I could win at Augusta. Either I need to play perfect golf and get lucky or I need it to rain all week so my low approaches will stick. I can't hit the ball a mile high like Jack and these other guys."

So for many years in the prime of his career, Trevino simply skipped the tournament. Then Nicklaus had a heart-to-heart with him one day.

"You don't know how good you really are," Nicklaus told him. "You can beat anyone on any course. The only person you're hurting by skipping Augusta is yourself."

The conversation did more than simply get Trevino to come to the Masters. It gave him a much-needed boost of confidence.

"There was never any doubt in my mind that Jack was the best player in the world, and probably the best that ever lived," Trevino said. "But one thing that made him so great is that he loved the challenge. He wanted you to play your best because he wanted to beat the best. If you beat him, fine. But at least you had to play your best to do it. What Jack said to me that day turned me around. He didn't have to do it, and it sure didn't do him any good, but that's the kind of champion he is."

Jack Nicklaus isn't above poking fun at himself, as he did at a dinner in 2000.

"I met a man the other day who had a dog that loved to watch golf on television," Nicklaus said. "He told me that the dog flipped head over heels whenever I made a par and flipped twice for birdies. I asked him what the dog did when I won and the man said he didn't know. He'd only had the dog for five years."

After playing with Tiger Woods in the first two rounds of the 2000 PGA Championship, Nicklaus offered Woods a sizable compliment.

"Tiger plays a game which I'm not familiar with," Nicklaus said, echoing a phrase Bobby Jones used to describe Nicklaus's game following his 1965 Masters victory. "Of course, I played a game I'm not familiar with either."

On the eve of the final round of the 1972 U.S. Open at Pebble Beach, Jack Nicklaus had a vivid nightmare. In his dream, he came to the par-3 17th with a three-stroke lead and hit his drive into one of the bunkers guarding the green. From that point until he awoke, he futilely played from one bunker to another and failed to finish the hole. The nightmare was so dramatic that Nicklaus couldn't go back to sleep.

Sure enough, when he came to the 17th on Sunday, he had a three-stroke lead. If the nightmare even entered his mind, it didn't seem to affect Nicklaus. His 1-iron hit the pin and landed inches from the hole, locking up his third U.S. Open title.

There's no question that equipment has improved dramatically in recent years, and this is particularly true when it comes to golf balls.

Not so very long ago, players on Tour would get a dozen balls from their manufacturer's rep and hope to find three or four that were worth using in competition.

How bad were some balls?

On the eve of the 2000 U.S. Open, the United States Golf Association checked some MacGregor Tourneys, the ball Jack Nicklaus played during the most productive years of his career.

According to the USGA tests, the ball went twenty yards shorter than comparable balls of the era, and one ball consistently flew to the right, while another flew to the left.

The USGA's verdict? The MacGregor Tourney might have been the worst golf ball ever made—which makes Jack Nicklaus's record all the more amazing.

Great players have a way of getting themselves into a zone of concentration where nothing but the shot at hand enters their mind. Jack Nicklaus did this as well or better than anyone else.

"You could tell Jack on the first tee that his house had burned down and he wouldn't think about it until he putted out of 18," Ken Venturi often observed.

Of course, sometimes his intensity produced comic moments.

In 1975, he began the final day of the Masters by striding purposefully out onto the practice tee—in his street shoes.

At the ceremony honoring Jack Nicklaus at the 2000 Memorial Tournament, Gary Player spoke for millions of golfers when he summed up why he thought Nicklaus has meant so much to the game of golf.

"A great coach once said that you show me a good loser and I'll show you a non-winner," Player said. "Well, Jack Nicklaus has defied that. He's the most gracious winner and loser in the history of the game."

FRANCIS OUIMET

Francis Ouimet, who won the 1913 U.S. Open and two U.S. Amateurs, is one of the most revered figures in American golf history, but his career almost ended before it had really begun.

As a young caddie he developed a love for the game and would get up in the early hours and sneak onto The Country Club, conveniently located across the street from his home in Brookline, Massachusetts. He was caught so many times by greens keepers that his mother made him promise to never do it again.

When he turned sixteen, he faced a dilemma. The Rules of Golf at that time declared that anyone who caddied past the age of sixteen was a professional golfer and therefore ineligible to compete in amateur competitions.

By this time he had begun to attract some local attention for his play, and was offered a junior membership at nearby Charles River Country Club. The fee was a princely twenty-five dollars—which Ouimet didn't have—so he asked if he might borrow the money from his mother.

"After much pleading, she eventually gave in but most reluctantly and insisted that I pay it back," Ouimet recalled years later. "She ended our conversation by saying she was certain golf was going to be the ruin of me."

Hardly.

ARNOLD PALMER

In the Saturday afternoon matches in the 1967 Ryder Cup, Arnold Palmer was paired with Julius Boros against Scotland's George Will and Ireland's Hugh Boyle. The Americans figured to have an easy time of it, but at the turn they were 4-down.

Not taking any chances that Palmer's noted competitiveness might not be enough to pull the team through, former Masters and PGA Champion Jackie Burke wandered out to rally the troops.

"Well, Arnold," Burke said. "I keep hearing about these famous charges of yours. Let's see if you can pull yourself out of this one."

That was all it took.

"OK, Jack, if that's how you want it, maybe we'll just do something about it," said Palmer.

"If you beat these guys, Arnold, I'll hand build you a clock," said Burke.

Palmer went out and won the 10th hole with a par and the 11th with a birdie. He reached the par-5 13th in two and won the hole with another birdie, then added a birdie on the 14th for good measure.

"I'll be damned if he didn't pull it out," said Burke after the match.

In the end, Palmer and Boros squeezed out a 1-up victory, which ran Palmer's record for the week to 5-0 as the Americans breezed to a 23½ to 8½ victory.

Today, the clock Burke had built sits in Palmer's club repair shop back home in Latrobe, Pennsylvania. Instead of numbers, the twelve letters of Arnold Palmer's name grace the face of the clock.

When the 1975 Ryder Cup Matches were played at Laurel Valley Golf Club near Palmer's boyhood home, it was only fitting that Palmer serve as captain of the United States team.

The Americans won by 10 points, and later Palmer was asked about his pairings.

Lee Trevino and J. C. Snead: "No one else but J. C. can play with Lee. He talks them all to death."

Hale Irwin and Gene Littler: "They're both quiet."

Johnny Miller and Al Geiberger: "They're both tall and they're both from California."

You might question Arnold's logic, but not the results.

After playing their rounds in the 2001 Tradition, Jack Nicklaus watched a frustrated Arnold Palmer hit balls on the practice tee.

"See anything?" Palmer asked Nicklaus.

"I think the problem is your address position," Nicklaus said, holding his forefinger out at an angle, and then turning it downward. "You start out fine but after a while you just sort of go like this."

"When you get to be my age, that's not the only part of your body that happens to," Palmer joked.

Dave Marr was paired with Arnold Palmer in the opening match of the 1965 Ryder Cup at Royal Birkdale.

While Palmer was already a veteran of the Matches, it was the first and only appearance for Marr, the winner of the 1965 PGA Championship, and he was as nervous as is humanly possible.

After hitting a series of truly horrible shots, he approached his partner.

"Arnold, I'm choking so bad," said Marr.

"Welcome to the Ryder Cup," Palmer said. "But don't apologize. I know you're trying."

It is hard to imagine a more disappointing moment in Arnold Palmer's career than the 1966 U.S. Open at San Francisco's Olympic Club.

Palmer led Billy Casper by seven strokes as they stood on the 10th tee in the final round. After losing the Open in playoffs in 1962 and '63, it seemed virtually certain he would win his second U.S. Open title.

But Palmer had something grander in mind. He knew he had a good shot at breaking Ben Hogan's 1948 Open record of 276, and besides, playing conservatively and protecting his lead was an alien concept to Palmer.

But catastrophe struck on the back nine and Casper caught Palmer and tied him after Palmer skied to a 39, setting up a playoff the following day.

Once again, Palmer came to the back nine with a lead, this time three strokes. And once again, he failed to hold it. This time it cost him the championship, as Casper won his second Open by shooting a 69 to Palmer's 73.

Palmer was understandably crushed by the loss, as was his caddie, a young man named Mike Reasor. As Palmer went to the awards ceremony, Reasor went to the locker room to wait for him.

"I could hear the speeches from the ceremony, and I couldn't believe that Arnold was praising me for the job I'd done," said Reasor. "It just showed what a classy guy he is. He took the loss with such dignity. He left the ceremony and headed for the clubhouse with his head held high. No one could have guessed how much it hurt him. But as soon as he came into the locker room and saw me, his head dropped and his chin just sagged. He came up, put his arm over my shoulder, and said, 'Sorry Mike.' I'll never forget that."

Arnold Palmer and Jack Nicklaus had a celebrated rivalry, both on and off the course, for much of their careers. In fact, both will admit that there were tournaments when they were paired together that they focused solely on beating each other's brains out, to the exclusion of the tournament proper.

While the rivalry was always civil, it occasionally got out of hand.

"One night we were sitting at a table and I kicked his shin," Nicklaus recalls. "He kicked me back and so I kicked him again. Neither one of us wanted to be the first to stop, so we nearly kicked ourselves until we were bloody. The next day we both had big, ugly bruises on our legs. It was just stupid. If your kids did it you'd think they were crazy."

The Palmer-Nicklaus rivalry may have cooled somewhat with time, but neither man can resist occasionally giving the other a dig if the opportunity presents itself.

Palmer created an enormous controversy late in 2000 when he endorsed a nonconforming—hence essentially illegal—driver made by his sponsor, Callaway. The debate divided the golf world into two camps: those who agreed that the vast majority of golfers should be able to use basically whatever equipment they wanted and those who believed there should be one set of rules for everyone.

At about this time, Palmer and Nicklaus were scheduled to play a round to celebrate the opening of The King and the Bear course at the World Golf Hall of Fame, their first collaborative design.

As they stood on the tee, Palmer looked over at Nicklaus's bag and asked him what kind of clubs he was playing.

"Legal ones," Nicklaus said, pointedly. "How about you?"

The King and the Bear hosted the 2001 Liberty Mutual Legends of Golf and the Nicklaus/Palmer collaboration met with almost universal praise from the toughest possible audience—their fellow pros.

"It's so good I don't think either one of them had anything to do with it," Lee Trevino joked.

Arnold Palmer and Jack Nicklaus were watching the telecast of the final round of the 2000 BellSouth Classic. Gary Nicklaus, a Tour rookie, had a chance to win and the two old friends and rivals were glued to the television.

Gary hit a good drive but faced a difficult second shot to an island green protected by water.

"Lay up, lay up," Palmer urged.

"You never laid up once in your career," Nicklaus said.

"Yeah," Palmer said. "Well, maybe if I had I would have beat you more often."

GARY PLAYER

When Gary Player arrived at Muirfield for the 1959 British Open, the bookies had him listed as a 6-to-1 shot at winning.

Player's fellow countryman Harold Henning took one look at the odds and one look at Player's form and put down a £100 bet.

Player won, and considering the purses in those days, that might have made Harold Henning the leading money winner for the week.

Gary Player isn't necessarily a superstitious man, but, on the other hand, he doesn't believe in tempting fate.

In the 1965 U.S. Open at Bellerive, he opened strongly in the first round and decided to wear the same shirt the next day. So when he returned to his hotel, he washed the shirt by hand and hung it up to dry overnight. He did the same thing after the second round. And the third round. And when he found himself tied with Australia's Kel Nagle after seventy-two holes, he went back and washed the shirt in preparation for the next day's playoff—which he won.

Even from an early age, Gary Player was fiercely determined to succeed.

One day his teacher awoke early in the morning. He could hear a voice in a nearby room, and decided to investigate. He discreetly looked into the room, where he saw Gary Player staring at his reflection in a mirror.

"I'm going to be the greatest player in the game's history," he heard Player say, and he heard him say it fifty times before he gave up counting.

When Player finished, he gathered up his clubs and went outside to practice bunker shots.

He was sixteen years old.

When Gary Player won the 1961 Masters, he became the first international player to win the coveted Green Jacket. He also became the first player to keep one.

"I wasn't aware of the rules and regulations and I naturally assumed that the Green Jacket was like a trophy, so I brought it home with me to South Africa," Player recalls. "Clifford Roberts called me and told me in no uncertain terms that the Green Jacket was not to leave the club grounds. I invited him to come to South Africa for a visit and he could bring it back. I don't think he was amused. He told me to just make sure and bring it back the following spring."

The Green Jacket never made it back.

"My father keeps it at home with his honors jacket from college," said Marc Player. "It's one of the things he fondly looks at when he reminisces about his life and career."

Gary Player was the first truly great golfer who exposed the importance of a healthy diet and physical fitness, although not everyone took him all that seriously.

"He'd finish his round and change into a sweat suit and go run around the course," remembers Lee Trevino. "We thought he was crazy. He'd come back to the clubhouse and we'd be in the bar having a beer (or possibly something stronger) and he'd come in and ask for an orange juice— without anything in it. I looked at him and said, 'You're killing me. Have a Bud.'"

On another occasion, he walked into a restaurant, spotted Trevino, took one look at the table, and threw the loaf of bread to the floor.

"What the hell are you doing?" Trevino asked. "That's my bread."

"No," said Player. "That's poison. That will kill you."

"Unless I starve first," said Trevino.

Jack Nicklaus thought so highly of Gary Player that he named one of his sons Gary. But even he had his doubts about Player's fitness claims.

"Gary," he said. "I've been thinking about this. If you worked out as much as you say you do, you wouldn't have time to do anything else."

When Jack Nicklaus was honored at the 2000 Memorial Tournament, Arnold Palmer, PGA Tour Commissioner Tim Finchem, and Gary Player were asked to give brief speeches. Player couldn't resist poking a little fun at his old friend.

"Jack has a reputation for being a little tardy at times," Player said. "I'm not saying that's true, but if one of my race-horses was that late to the finish line he would have been shot."

Then he took note of Jack's prodigious appetite.

"Dining out with Jack could be a risky business," Player said. "The man is no slouch with a knife and fork. In fact, if you weren't careful he'd butter your hand."

POLS

Politicians today have no qualms about being photographed playing golf. Indeed, for many of them it is a passion. But this was not always the case. Teddy Roosevelt, for one, took pains to avoid any association with the game when he was in the White House.

"I play tennis, but you'll never see a photograph of me playing," he told a friend. "I'm careful about how I'm photographed. Tennis, no, but anything on horseback, yes. Golf? Never. That's fatal."

Richard Nixon was never much of a golfer, or much of an athlete for that matter. He played a bit when he was vice president, largely because President Dwight Eisenhower was so passionate about the game.

One weekend during his own presidency, he visited Camp David. He ran into Henry Kissinger, then his National Security Advisor.

"I scored a 126," he said.

"That's very good, Mr. President," said Kissinger. "Your golf is certainly improving."

"I was bowling, Henry," Nixon replied.

Al Smith, the great Democratic governor of New York who was the first Irish-Catholic to run for president, had an interesting approach to golf.

If he was in a tight match, he would build little mounds of sand and then tee up his shots from the fairway.

"How can you do that?" asked Hugh Carey, another former governor of the state. "It's against the rules."

"First, I can do it because the sand is part of the course," Smith said. "And second, I can do it because I'm the governor."

Hugh Carey was fond of telling the story about the time he played with Bob Hope.

"We had what was known as the 'Battle of the One-Liners' when I was in Albany," Carey recalled. "He said 'Now I know why the State of New York has a budget office. They keep score for the governor.'"

THE PRESS

Australia's Stuart Appleby was playing in the 2000 Compaq Classic of New Orleans at the English Turn Golf & Country Club.

On the 12th hole, he hit his ball into a water hazard and elected to play the ball from the mud. The good news was that he got the ball back safely into play. The bad news was that he was covered with mud.

When he finished his round, he headed for the locker room to wash up and change his clothes. Guarding the clubhouse door was one Sgt. George Hurban of the New Orleans Police Department, who hesitated before letting Appleby into the clubhouse.

"I took one look at the guy and just assumed he was a writer," said Hurban. "I was going to ask him which paper he worked for when I saw his player's badge."

Anyone who ever spent much time around a pressroom could understand Hurban's confusion.

One year at the U.S. Open, word filtered through the press-room that a veteran writer was suffering from Lyme disease.

"The only way that's true is if you get it from bad limes," a fellow writer quipped.

Today, golf coverage is an important part of any sports section, but this wasn't always the case. When Francis Ouimet won the 1913 U.S. Open, the publisher of the *New York Evening Mail* approached his editor and asked why the paper didn't cover golf.

"What's golf?" the editor answered.

"My God, man, it's an important sport," the publisher said. "All my friends play it. It's very popular among businessmen."

"Then put it on the financial pages," the editor grumbled.

While most writers adhere to a certain loosely interpreted code of journalistic ethics, matters like free rounds of golf, press junkets, etc. occasionally prove too tempting for mere mortals. Take the case of the old-timer who showed up at a popular resort and asked for a starting time. No problem, until the dicey matter of the greens fee was brought up.

"Greens fee!" he harrumphed. "I've never paid for a round of golf in my life and I don't intend to start now."

Thus fortified with righteous indignation, he left. One can only imagine what he wrote about the place.

THE ROYAL & ANCIENT GOLF CLUB OF ST. ANDREWS

Tony Lema won the 1964 British Open at The Old Course at St. Andrews, but his first reaction to the place was less than enthusiastic.

"Jim," he said to ABC announcer Jim McKay. "We have an island back home in San Francisco that's better suited for golf than this place. It's called Alcatraz."

THE RULES

Ian Woosnam's brush with the fourteen-club rule in the 2001 British Open brought into focus a rule with one of the most interesting histories in the game.

Until the mid-1930s, there was no limit to the number of clubs a player could have in his bag. For example, Lawson Little had thirty-one clubs in his bag when he won the 1934 and 1935 U.S. and British Amateurs. In 1935, the United States Golf Association surveyed contestants in the U.S. Open and found they averaged eighteen clubs per bag.

In part, this was because players were making the switch from hickory to steel shafts, but had certain favorite old clubs they kept for playing certain shots—or maybe just as confidence builders.

So how did the USGA and the R&A settle on fourteen clubs?

No one is quite sure, but one school of thought traces the decision back to a conversation between Bobby Jones and Tony Torrance, a veteran of several British/Irish Walker Cup teams.

Jones said that when he won the Grand Slam in 1930 he carried sixteen clubs. Torrance said he never carried more than twelve. Fourteen seemed a worthy compromise.

Still, if a two-stroke penalty seems a bit draconian, consider this: the original penalty was disqualification—which happened to a contestant in the 1955 British Amateur at Royal Lytham.

Halfway through the final round of the 1972 U.S. Open at Pebble Beach, two people protesting the war in Vietnam chained themselves to a tree in the 18th fairway. Since they weren't interfering with play, the decision was made to let them continue their protest.

As each group of players came to the 18th tee, they were informed of the protest and went about their business. When Arnold Palmer came to the tee, he asked to borrow a pair of binoculars so he could check out the situation. Naturally, since it was Arnold Palmer, ABC Sports cut to a shot of him gazing down the fairway.

The next day, the USGA's headquarters was swamped with phone calls from would-be Rules experts, demanding to know why Palmer wasn't penalized for using an "artificial device" during his round.

Some people simply have too much spare time on their hands.

Ted Bishop from Massachusetts met Smiley Quick in the finals of the 1946 U.S. Amateur at Baltusrol Golf Club. It was the first Amateur played following World War II and it attracted more press attention than usual, including an unusually large number of newsreel cameramen.

The sound of the cameras bothered Quick, but since Bishop was extremely hard of hearing, they didn't seem to have any effect on his play. Finally, Quick had enough and demanded the cameras be removed.

"Ted can't hear them because he's almost deaf, but I can," Quick complained.

The gallery apparently agreed, and began to agitate against the cameramen. Finally, with the match tied after thirty-five holes, the match's referee had seen—and heard—enough.

"If there's one more outburst in favor of Mr. Quick, I will forfeit the match in Mr. Bishop's favor," he warned the gallery.

Both players missed putts for the win on the final green and the match moved to a sudden-death playoff, which Bishop won on the next hole when Quick missed a 2½-footer for a halve.

Jack Nicklaus is a stickler for playing by the Rules. That may be because of a lesson he learned playing in the 1953 U.S. Junior Championship at Southern Hills Country Club in Tulsa, Oklahoma.

Playing his first round match, he ambled to the first tee a mere thirty seconds prior to his starting time.

"Mr. Nicklaus," said the starter to the thirteen-year old. "If you had waited another thirty seconds you would have been 1-down."

Bobby Jones was playing in the 1919 Southern Amateur—a huge event in those days, largely because Bobby Jones played in it. Jones, who was the defending champion, hit a poor drive in the first round of match play and incredibly, it bounced into a wheelbarrow and rolled into a shoe.

Jones asked the official for a ruling, and was told he had to play it or take a drop and a one-stroke penalty.

Jones studied the shot and decided to take his chances. He whacked the shoe and to his amazement—and to the amazement of his opponent and the gallery, both the shoe and the ball landed on the green. From that point, Jones two-putted for one of the greatest pars of all time.

ANNE QUAST SANDER

Anne Quast Sander is one of the greatest amateurs in American golf history. She won three U.S. Women's Amateurs—and doubtlessly would have won many, many more if her career hadn't coincided with that of "The Great Gundy"—JoAnne Gunderson Carner. She also won four Senior Women's Amateurs.

None of this, of course, impressed certain members of the male species in the British Isles.

She and her first husband, David Welts, lived in the United Kingdom for a time and had arranged to play Muirfield through the secretary at their local club.

On the day prior to their visit, she had set a new women's course record at the impossibly difficult Carnoustie, where Ben Hogan, Tom Watson, and Gary Player—among other Hall of Famers—won the British Open.

The story made all the Scottish papers, and upon their arrival, the starter looked at the daunting combination of both an American and a woman and asked her husband, "Can she play?"

Before he could answer, the starter looked down at the newspaper spread open before him. He studied the picture. He looked at the suspect in question.

"One o'clock," he said, tersely.

SHOW BUSINESS

Victor Mature once had a friend sound out some members of the membership committee at Los Angeles Country Club about his chances of joining. Several days later, the friend called him with some bad news.

"Sorry, Victor," his friend said. "They just don't accept actors."

"Then they've never seen my movies," Mature said. "I'm no actor, and I've got the films to prove it."

SAM SNEAD

When Sam Snead traveled to St. Andrews for the 1946 British Open, he figured that the trip alone cost him $2,000, which his winner's prize of $600 didn't begin to cover. When asked if he would come back the following year to defend his title, he was incredulous.

"Are you kidding?" he said.

But he did come back many years later and won the British Seniors Championship—and the princely sum of $460.

"They handed me the check and I asked the guy if this was my tipping money," Sam recalled. "When they told me that was the purse, I told them 'Don't call me. I'll call you.'"

Sam Snead has never really received the credit he deserves for being one of the keenest students of the golf swing that ever lived—as former British Open and Masters champion Nick Faldo discovered when he sought Sam out for advice early in 2000.

"I looked at Sam, with the greatest golf swing of the last century, and thought to myself that I was crazy not to ask

him for some help," said Faldo. "I thought it would be great to pick his brain and get some of the real key thoughts of how he played."

Earlier in his career, when Faldo was in the midst of reworking the swing that had made him the best player in the world, Sam had taken him aside at the Masters and tried to talk him out of it.

"Back home in Hot Springs, we might not be the smartest people in the world, but we do know that if something ain't broke, don't waste your time trying to fix it," Sam told him. "And a fella at your level shouldn't be taking advice from every Tom, Dick, and Harry. Go to someone who knows what it's like to play under the gun."

Several years later, when Faldo finally went to see Sam, the Slammer looked at tapes of Faldo in his prime, and then watched him hit a few drivers.

"He hit a couple drives that kind of tailed off to the right," Sam said. "Usually I can go right to the spot there, and that is the left hand. I gave him a little change to make there, and also had him narrow his stance a little bit. I told him you can't use your body in the swing if your feet are that wide apart. He drew them up about six inches and pretty soon he was hitting the prettiest little draws you've ever seen."

Later, Faldo asked Sam what he thought about when he was playing badly.

"I never played badly enough to think about it," Sam said, logically enough.

Naturally, given Tiger Woods's remarkable 2000 season, writers were anxious to learn what Sam Snead thought about the young man.

"Well, one day I was in California and his dad asked me if I'd play a few holes with Tiger," Sam recalled. "He had that same long, fast swing he has today but I don't think he should change it. That's just what's natural for him and you can't work against Mother Nature. People say it will hurt him but I don't think so. He's been doing it since he was about six years old. His body's used to it by now."

George Plimpton once did a profile of Sam, and he came across a story about Sam that had been largely overlooked by the mainstream press.

"Sam used to claim he could lift a woman up and accurately guess her weight," Plimpton reported. "I interviewed one woman and asked her how close Sam came. 'Five pounds,' she said. That's when I realized what a cagey guy he was. It just gave him an excuse to get his hands on these beautiful young women."

For decades, people have written about Sam's love affair with a buck, and how he hated to part with one. But in truth, Sam could be very generous to people he knew and trusted.

"When Porky Oliver came out on Tour he was always running into money trouble," Sam's friend Bob Goalby once recalled. "Sam would give him a blank check, but asked him to keep it under five figures."

"People ask about how accurate Sam was," recalls longtime friend Bobby Fry. "We used to go out to a driving range and he had a great bet. He'd tell you to go out to the 250-yard marker and he'd bet you that he could hit five balls and make you move at least once."

Sam and Audrey Snead's youngest son, Terry, is mentally retarded and has been institutionalized for much of his life. One time he visited Sam in Philadelphia. When it was time for Terry to leave, he was distraught.

"Daddy, please don't go," he pleaded.

"It broke Sam's heart," recalls his friend Johnny Bulla. "He began to cry and said 'I'd give everything I have if I could just help him. There's so much I want to do for him and I can't do a thing.'"

"One time when Terry was visiting, Sam took him when he went to practice," recalls a friend, Bobby Fry. "Terry would sit there watching Sam and at one point, just as he was about to hit, the ball fell off the tee.

"'Strike three,' Terry said.

"Sam got the biggest kick out of that," Fry said.

When the Senior PGA Tour was just getting its start, Sam and some other players met with Ben Hogan and tried to talk him into playing, or at least making token appearances. Finally, Hogan had heard enough and slammed his fist down on a table.

"My game is not for public display," he said.

"Well then, Ben, I guess I'll have to play them all," said Sam Snead. And he basically did.

Sam Snead was playing England's Harry Weetman in the 1953 Ryder Cup Matches at Wentworth Golf Club. He had a comfortable lead with five holes to play but unaccountably let it slip away.

Playing the 13th hole, he hit a poor drive and made a double bogey to lose the hole. Weetman hit a remarkable chip on the next hole and further trimmed Sam's lead. Poor drives on the next two holes cost Sam his lead altogether. Weetman birdied the 17th hole to take the lead and when they halved the 18th, Weetman had staged one of the greatest comebacks in Ryder Cup history and Snead had suffered his first loss.

"It was tough but it taught me a good lesson," Snead admitted. "Never collect any trophies in your head until you have them in your hand."

Sam Snead had already won the Greater Greensboro Open seven times when he arrived at the tournament in 1965.

At a pretournament dinner in his honor, host Ed Sullivan asked the gathering how great it would be if Sam, at age fifty-three, won for an eighth time. They roared their approval.

"It gave me a little jolt and I thought I'd make a little extra effort," Sam recalled.

He got another jolt when a young Raymond Floyd was quoted as saying that while it was great that Sam was at the tournament, he didn't have a chance of winning.

Not only did Sam win by four strokes, but he cut Floyd by eleven.

Lee Trevino once called Sam Snead "the greatest athlete in American history" and 1968 Masters Champion Bob Goalby has a story to back up that claim.

"One day when Sam was in his fifties Gary Player challenged him to a footrace," Goalby recalls. "They took off their shoes and socks and off they went. Sam was pretty well ahead when Gary pulled up lame. Sam loved it."

Sam Snead isn't outwardly religious, but he isn't above asking for the occasional divine intervention.

"One day Sam and I were paired together in the old North and South Open," recalls his longtime friend Johnny Bulla.

"Sam made a 7 on a hole and while he was waiting to tee off on the next hole he looked to the heavens and said, 'Lord, why are you so mean to Sambo? I don't drink. I don't smoke. You're not mad 'cause I like the girls are you?'"

PAYNE STEWART

Payne Stewart died in an October 25, 1999, plane crash, just four months after winning his second U.S. Open. Six years earlier, he had come to the Pebble Beach Golf Links as the Open's defending champion.

Before the 1992 U.S. Open, he visited Pebble Beach and was sitting in the Tap Room with his friend and teacher, Chuck Cook, talking to a man who didn't recognize Stewart—the defending champion—without his knickers and trademark cap. Finally, Stewart found a clever way to convince the man that he was, in fact, the one and only Payne Stewart.

"I'll go get the U.S. Open trophy, but only if you promise to fill it with champagne," Stewart said.

The man agreed, and a few minutes later, the trophy was filled to the brim with expensive champagne.

"That might be the only guy who was ever sorry he met Payne Stewart," Cook recalled later.

Thinking back on his memories of that night, Chuck Cook had a special plan in mind when he returned to Pebble Beach for the 2000 U.S. Open.

"I'm going to take a bottle of champagne down to the seawall on 18 where Payne and I sat that night," says Cook. "I'm going to sit there and talk to my friend about life."

Payne Stewart would have been the defending champion when the U.S. Open returned to Pebble Beach in 2000. To honor his memory, two groups of golfers—forty in all—hit drives into the Pacific in a Wednesday morning ceremony.

Jack Nicklaus, who was assigned the defending champion's traditional starting time, decided to remember Stewart in a slightly more private but even more moving manner.

Nicklaus stood behind his ball on the first tee, his head bowed in a moment of silence. Then he began to walk toward the ball and assume his address position, only to pause and walk to his bag, where he wiped the tears from his eyes with a towel.

"I wanted to give Payne a moment of silence but I didn't expect it would be that emotional," Nicklaus said later. "I just couldn't focus on the shot."

TEMPER, TEMPER

One day a man came into the clubhouse and asked the bartender for some ice to put on his swollen eye.

"Good God, sir," the bartender said. "What happened to you?"

"I got into an argument over the Rules and was punched," the man said.

"Well, I hope you punched him back," the bartender said.

"I did no such thing," the man said, walking away.

"I'll keep that in mind," the bartender said to a nearby waitress. "I've wanted to smack him for years."

JIM THORPE

There are very few African-American golfers on the Senior PGA Tour, so you'd think that they would be pretty identifiable, but that's not always the case.

When Jim Thorpe was about to tee off in the first round of the 2001 Senior PGA Championship, the announcer introduced him to the gallery as Jim Dent.

Thorpe stepped away from his ball and joked to the man "Do all of us look alike to you?"

LEE TREVINO

"One time I was paired with Lee Trevino and Tom Watson," remembers Roger Maltbie. "We had an early starting time and got to the practice tee just as the sun was coming up. We hit a few balls and Tom said to Lee, 'Mex, you think you can hit that 100-yard sign out there?'

"'Hell, which part of the sign do you want me to hit?' Trevino asked.

"'Hit the right "O,"' Watson said.

"He hit it with the first shot," Maltbie said. "People were falling down laughing.

"'It doesn't take long to warm up a Rolls-Royce,' Trevino said."

HARRY VARDON

As Bobby Jones began to make his mark on the game, writers were anxious to learn what Harry Vardon thought of the young man. Vardon, who won a record six British Opens and a U.S. Open, was admirably hesitant to offer an opinion. The two were paired in the 1920 U.S. Open, however, and Vardon finally offered his thoughts to the press.

"The youngster is a fine player," Vardon said. "He has a sound style and the possibilities of his game impressed me enormously."

"Is he better than Francis Ouimet or Chick Evans?" a writer persisted.

"I said he's a fine golfer, isn't that quite enough?" Vardon replied, testily.

BOBBY WADKINS

Bobby Wadkins, the younger brother of Lanny Wadkins, never enjoyed his brother's success on the PGA Tour. Although he enjoyed a respectable career, he never managed to win, although he did have six second-place finishes.

But as his fiftieth birthday approached, he went to work on his game, particularly his wedge play, and it paid off when he won his first senior tournament, the Lightpath Long Island Classic. His victory brought back memories of his last runner-up finish, the 1994 Kemper Open.

Wadkins began the final round with a one-stroke lead over Mark Brookes. They were tied when they reached the par-5 6th hole, but Wadkins, going for the green in two, pushed his second shot into the trees, lost his ball, and made an 8. He wound up losing by three strokes to Brookes.

Later, when a writer reminded him that even though he'd lost, he'd made enough money to be exempt from qualifying the following year, Wadkins took small comfort.

"You know, I'd give away every cent of that check and the exemption if I could just once have the feeling Mark has now," Wadkins said. "All I want to do, just once in my life, is hold up that trophy on Sunday afternoon and say 'I beat everyone, I'm the champion.' I'd like to do it just once."

It was a long wait, but he finally did.

TOM WATSON

People can and will debate forever which was the greatest round of golf ever played, but one that is almost always mentioned is the 69 in the second round on Tom Watson's way toward winning the 1979 Memorial Tournament.

The conditions were close to unplayable. With winds blowing in gusts over thirty miles per hour, the windchill was figured at 15 below zero. The scoring average for the day was an astronomical 78.738, and forty-two players failed to even break 80.

In typical Watson fashion, he said later that it was one of the most enjoyable and satisfying rounds he ever played.

Satisfying? OK. Enjoyable? You've got to be either kidding or Tom Watson.

One of the most dramatic shots in U.S. Open history was Tom Watson's chip in from the rough on the 17th hole in the 1982 Open at Pebble Beach. The shot allowed him to beat Jack Nicklaus, who was watching on television near the 18th green.

Over the years, Nicklaus rarely asked Watson about the shot, but in 2000 when the Open returned to Pebble Beach, the two were paired in a practice round.

When they reached the 17th green, Nicklaus asked Watson where his ball had come to rest. Watson showed him the spot, but hastened to add the lie was almost impossibly perfect.

"When Jack saw that the lie made the shot a little simpler it made it easier for him," Watson said. "Also, the pain isn't as intense after eighteen years."

THE WILD KINGDOM

Even wild animals occasionally seem to sense when they are in the presence of greatness.

One year at a tournament in New Orleans, Jack Nicklaus was preparing to hit a very difficult putt. One of the marshals near the green held up a sign that read "Quiet" to silence the gallery. That was fine, except for the group of ducks that were happily quacking away in a nearby pond.

Given Nicklaus's remarkable powers of concentration, it's unlikely he would have even noticed the ducks, but the marshal wasn't taking any chances. He turned to the ducks and pointed the sign at them.

The ducks immediately fell silent and swam away.

When Arnold Palmer made his record-breaking flight around the world, he was forced to make a landing in Sri Lanka in the middle of the night to refuel. To make matters worse, he was tired and the landing field was fogged in. Still, he had no choice.

Happily, Palmer landed the plane safely and taxied toward the terminal. When the plane had safely stopped, he opened the door to find a huge crowd of well-wishers and, of all things, an elephant waiting to take him to the capital to present trophies to the winners of national tournaments.

Palmer being Palmer, he was delighted, mounted the elephant for the twenty-minute ride to the capital, and returned in time to take off in pursuit of his record.

A very proper British club was split over a proposal to ban dogs from the course. In the course of the debate, one old member vowed to resign if the measure passed.

"I wouldn't dream of belonging to a club that bans dogs," he said. "And as a practical matter, I couldn't afford to belong if my Lab was banned. He is uncanny at finding golf balls. I haven't purchased a ball in ten years, and if I have to start now I shall be in the poorhouse."

A visiting officer on leave from Vietnam was enjoying a round of golf at a course near the Clark Air Force Base in the Philippines. On one of the closing holes, he hit his approach shot close to the hole, but as he approached the green, he spotted an enormous cobra sunning itself near his ball, with no apparent interest in leaving.

"What do I do now?" the officer asked his playing partner.

"You can either putt the ball or invoke the 'Cobra Rule,'" the man said.

"What's that?" the officer asked.

"Leave the ball for the snake, take a two-stroke penalty, and consider yourself lucky," the man said.

Harry Truman once famously noted that if you want a friend in Washington, get a dog.

To a lesser degree, the same could be said for the nomadic life on the LPGA Tour.

At the players' dinner prior to the start of the 1994 Solheim Cup, all the competitors were asked to stand and explain what competing for the Cup meant to them.

"This is something I will tell my grandchildren about someday," Kelly Robbins said.

"Hey, Kelly, you're not even married yet," Michelle McGann called out.

"Well, then I'll tell my dog," Robbins said.

HERBERT WARREN WIND

Herbert Warren Wind is universally recognized as one of the finest golf writers in a field that has produced a remarkably high number of stylists. His pieces for *The New Yorker* and *Sports Illustrated* inspired generations of young writers.

Herb Wind grew up in Brockton, Massachusetts, graduated from Yale University, and then studied at Cambridge University. His time in England allowed him to play the classic courses of the British Isles, read writers such as Bernard Darwin, and even compete in the British Amateur.

"Herb went over there as an American student and came back as a British writer," observed his longtime friend Charlie Yates, a member at Augusta National and former British Amateur champion. "He was cut from the mold of those fine golf writers from Scotland and England. He had such a love for the game and an appreciation for it."

Wind's love and passion for the game was embodied in his long friendship with Bob Jones, the player and man he held in the highest regard.

"The game has been blessed by great champions," Wind has often said. "Sarazen, Ouimet, Palmer, Player, Nicklaus, Trevino, Watson—my word, such great champions and so respectful of the game."

But when pressed, he allows that Jones was the supreme champion.

"Bob Jones," he says. "My goodness, what a brilliant, wonderful man."

Wind's boyhood love for the game was fueled by Jones's weekly radio show.

"Bob had a show with Grantland Rice, and we huddled around the radio every Friday night to learn about golf," Wind recalled fondly. "They were marvelous shows, so informative. They were educators, really, and they taught me so much about the game."

Wind's friendship with Jones bonded in 1947 when *The New Yorker* assigned him to profile the great champion.

"I made a lunch date with him at his law office, assuming that he'd be more comfortable there because he was already suffering the effects of syringomyelia, the disease that crippled him and eventually took his life in 1971. Instead, he insisted on going out for lunch. He was so dignified. He never let the discomfort stop him."

"Of all the people I have met in sports—or out of sports— Jones came closest to being what we call a 'Great Man,'" Wind said. "Like Winston Churchill, Bob ['Always Bob to his friends and Bobby to his fans,' Wind often pointed out] had the quality of at once being larger than life and yet exceedingly human. Jones had a remarkably fine mind and an astonishing memory."

Herb Wind will always be identified with the Masters and Augusta National, if only because he is credited with coining the name "Amen Corner" for the 11th, 12th, and 13th holes. The year was 1958, and in his piece for *Sports Illustrated* he wrote "down in the Amen Corner where Rae's Creek intersects the 13th fairway near the tee, then parallels the front edge of the green on the short 12th and finally swirls alongside the 11th green." Wind then went on to describe how that year's champion, Arnold Palmer, played the holes in defeating Ken Venturi.

"I took the term from the old jazz song 'Shouting at the Amen Corner,' Wind explained. "Imagine that it became part of golf lore."

Over the years, when Wind arrived in Augusta for the Masters, he was famous for asking the first friend or writer he encountered "Tell me, how are the greens?" He was also known for his sense of style and decorum. No matter how hot and humid it was, he would turn out in a proper tweed jacket, shirt, and tie.

Indeed, in 2001, when he was eighty-five and hadn't been to the Masters in ten years, he sat down with Jim McCabe, the fine young golf writer from the *Boston Globe*.

Toward the end of the interview, he said, "Tell me, is Augusta still beautiful?" I assured him that it was and he said, "Good, that pleases me. Bob would be pleased, too."

WIVES, LOVERS, AND OTHER STRANGERS

When the PGA Championship came to Winged Foot Golf Club in 1997, a man invited a young woman he had just begun dating to attend the final round of the tournament with him. Since she knew virtually nothing about golf, she asked some friends for advice. One thing she learned was that it was easy to identify the players, since they all have their names written on their golf bags.

Everything went along swimmingly until late in the afternoon the final group approached the green where they were sitting.

"Oh, look," she said, pointing to Justin Leonard. "It's Ben Hogan. He's very famous."

A woman was playing in an interclub match in one of the Boston suburbs. Whenever she hit a poor shot, she said, "There's another son-in-law shot." Finally, her opponent asked her what she meant.

"It's what my father calls any shot that doesn't turn out the way he hoped it would," she said.

The next two stories are almost certainly the figment of someone's imagination (we can only hope), but are well worth sharing.

A man was playing in a member-guest tournament at one of the prominent clubs in the New York City suburbs. He and his partner finished their round and had several drinks. The combination of the alcohol and the heat and humidity made the guest woozy, and when he went into the locker room to shower and dress for dinner, he became disoriented and somehow wound up in the women's locker room.

He started to leave, but since there was a line of men waiting to shower and the women's locker room was empty, he decided to take his chances and go ahead and shower.

Bad decision.

Everything went fine until he stepped out of the shower and began toweling off his hair—just as three women walked in.

"How disgusting," the first said. "A man in our locker room."

"He's not even covered up," said the second.

"He's not even a member," said the third.

One day following a club tournament, the phone rang in the crowded men's grill at a club outside Chicago. After several rings, a man finally walked over and answered it.

"Well, $25,000 for a bracelet does seem like a lot of money, but if you like it, honey, that's fine," the man said.

There was a pause while he listened for a minute.

"A million-five is a stretch, but if you like the house and the broker thinks it's a bargain, go ahead," he said, and then listened a bit longer.

"Sure, what the hell," he said. "I think the twins deserve matching BMWs. Whatever color you want is fine with me. Okay, dear. Good-bye."

He hung up the phone and returned to the bar.

"Anyone know who that call was for?" he asked.

In January 2000, there was a party at the Nicklaus home to celebrate Jack's sixtieth birthday. The most inspired gift was from Raymond and Maria Floyd: a book titled *Sex After 60*.

Jack paged through it and called to his wife, Barbara.

"You have to read this," he said.

"I don't have time," she said, blushing.

"You'll have time," Jack said, handing her the book—filled with blank pages.

Ben and Valerie Hogan were married for sixty-two years. She was the love of his life, and they were utterly devoted to each other, almost from the time they met as children growing up in Fort Worth.

"Ben was always my mother's favorite of all the boys who came around," she recalled after his death. "He had wonderful manners, which appealed to her, but he was also very charming. He'd come to the house for a visit, and when he'd leave, she'd say, 'Valerie, that little Ben Hogan is the nicest fellow who comes to this house,' and Ben was that way his whole life."

The Hogans knew good times and bad times. He went broke at least three times before finding success on Tour. He was nearly killed in a car accident, but came back to become one of the game's greatest champions and most inspirational figures. Still, the one constant was his devotion to his wife.

"He always gave of himself for me," she remembered. "He hated to see me upset. If he saw that I was, he'd come and take me by the hand. 'Let's sit down and let that go. Let's talk about it,' he'd say to me, and sure enough, things would be all right."

Ben Hogan's fascination with the game and the swing was something he carried with him all the time, both on the course and off. He was constantly thinking about ways to improve, trying to find all the answers to a game that constantly poses new questions for even the greatest players.

One evening, Valerie Hogan asked her husband a simple question.

"Ben, why don't you just give that brain of yours a rest?" she said.

"Valerie, if you don't keep using it, it will go to pot," he replied. "There are nine jillion things to learn about the golf swing and I don't think anyone will ever really understand it. I've just scratched the surface. It's a very complex thing, you know."

No doubt, she knew better than most people.

When you look at great golfers, one common denominator is a long and successful marriage. That is certainly the case with Jack Nicklaus—as he pointed out during a ceremony honoring him at the 2000 Memorial Tournament.

"Success is often all about timing, and that's certainly true in the game of golf," Nicklaus said, as his wife, Barbara, looked on. "I can say with absolute conviction that my timing was never better than on that day in 1957, outside Mendenhall Lab on the campus of Ohio State University, when I met Barbara Jean Bash. If it weren't for Barbara, I would have been just another golfer."

How important is a good marriage? According to the great golf writer Dan Jenkins, it's crucial. Take the case of Tiger Woods.

"There's only two things that can stop Tiger now," Jenkins said after Woods's phenomenal 2000 season. "An injury or a bad marriage."

Jack and Barbara Nicklaus began dating as freshmen at Ohio State and it wasn't long before she decided that if this was going to be the man in her life, she'd better learn a little bit about playing golf. She took a course in golf at school but was understandably apprehensive when they played for the first time.

She bogeyed the first hole—no small accomplishment, come to think of it.

"This game doesn't seem so hard, Jack," she said. "I don't understand why you think you have to practice so much."

TIGER WOODS

Anyone who doubts Tiger Woods's discipline and total self-control didn't watch him play the 18th hole in the final round of the 2000 Bell Canadian Open.

Leading Grant Waite by a stroke, he addressed the ball in front of the enormous gallery, which was totally, almost eerily, silent. He drew the club away from the ball, and in the midst of his downswing, someone in the gallery shouted, "Go Tiger!"

Woods stopped in mid-swing, the club head going from 120-plus miles per hour to zero in a split second.

Just the physical act alone is almost impossible to comprehend, never mind being able to do it on the final hole of a tournament.

Following his remarkable 2000 season, when he won the U.S. and British Opens and the PGA Championship, a writer asked Tiger Woods if that was his greatest year.

"No, when I was eleven I made straight "A's," won about thirty-two junior tournaments, had two recesses a day, and

had the cutest girlfriend in the whole school," he said. "Everything has been downhill since then."

Tiger Woods, Vijay Singh, and Jack Nicklaus were paired in the 2000 PGA Championship. On the opening hole, the gallery was ten deep in spots and after the players hit, they erupted in an enormous roar.

"I'm glad I'm done playing," Nicklaus said to Woods. "You've got to deal with this for the rest of your career."

In the same tournament they were playing the par-3 8th hole. Woods hit a 9-iron to ten feet. Nicklaus hit a 6-iron, his ball actually striking Woods's ball.

"Tiger," Nicklaus said. "Turn your club upside down so it looks like we hit the same club."

BABE ZAHARIAS

That Babe Zaharias was the greatest female athlete in history is pretty much beyond dispute. That she was instrumental in getting the LPGA up and running is also indisputable. But that she was universally loved is another matter.

The truth of the matter is that while she was phenomenally popular both in this country and in Great Britain, she ruffled more than her share of feathers among her fellow golfers—not that it seemed to bother her in the slightest.

At the root of the problem was her attitude. She was brash, cocky, arrogant, and outspoken. That she was also beating the other players like a drum and getting most of the publicity only added to the friction.

"If you want everyone to like you, finish thirtieth," Amy Alcott once famously observed, and the Babe wasn't about finishing thirtieth. In all, she won thirty-one LPGA events including ten major championships.

Paying the top golfers appearance fees to play in tournaments is commonplace around the world but is rare in the

174

United States—although players get around this by agreeing to perform a clinic during the tournament week for which they are handsomely compensated. This wasn't the case with the Babe, however. She demanded and received hefty appearance fees and wasn't the least bit shy about bragging about it. Naturally, this infuriated the other players, which was simply icing on the cake for the Babe.

"I'm the star," she frequently pointed out to her fellow pros. "You're just the chorus."

This attitude led the Babe to demand—and usually receive—special treatment.

In one tournament, she and Patty Berg were dueling head-to-head in the final round. Babe was off her game and Berg, an intense but cheerful competitor, had her on the ropes.

With just a few holes remaining, it began to rain lightly. The rain continued steadily and so did Berg's domination. Finally, the Babe had had enough. She stormed into the clubhouse and told the tournament sponsors that the course was unplayable and demanded that the round be canceled and rescheduled for the next day. She threatened that if it was not, she was withdrawing. Naturally, they relented.

Berg was furious. The rest of the players were furious. The Babe was thrilled.

Just to prove, however, that there is a certain justice to this game, the next day Berg went out and cleaned the Babe's clock—much to the delight of the other players.

One player who took a particularly dim view of Babe and her antics was Louise Suggs, a Hall of Famer in her own right. Among the catalogue of things that bothered Suggs was Babe's casual interpretation of the rules. On more than one occasion, Suggs simply refused to sign the Babe's score-card because of a rules violation—perceived or otherwise.

"Let's just say that Babe played by the rules, but just barely," Suggs said.

When the Babe won the 1947 Ladies' British Open Amateur Championship, she became the first American to win the championship since its inception in 1893.

The reserved Scots who turned out at Gullane didn't know what to make of the Babe at first blush, but they grew to adore her.

In one of her early matches, she became frustrated by what she took as a lack of enthusiasm by the Scots.

"Let's have some fun," she told the gallery. "Make all the noise you want. It will make me play better. I can't play when it's this quiet. I feel like I'm at a funeral."

After closing out a Mrs. Enid Sheppard in an afternoon match, 4 & 2, she asked if she could play the remaining two "bye" holes, as was traditional in America.

Naturally, the Babe being the Babe, it wasn't enough that she simply played the holes. Instead, she had to put on an exhibition.

On the 17th hole, she teed up her ball and then stuck a kitchen match in the ground behind the ball.

"When I hit the ball it sounded like a cannon going off because the match fires with a loud pop," the Babe told reporters. "I hit it about three hundred yards and the gallery went wild. The ball ended up in a bunker and I did another one of my tricks. I balanced one ball on top of the other. Then I hit the bottom ball. It went on the green and into the hole and the top ball popped up into the air and I caught it in my pocket. On the 18th green, I turned my back to the hole and putted the ball between my legs and right into the hole. They'd never seen anything like it. I was signing autographs for an hour."

The next day there was a sign posted in the clubhouse asking competitors to refrain from playing the bye holes. Apparently not everyone was thrilled by the Babe's act.

The Babe didn't know what to make of the ancient Scottish caddies. Her caddie for the 1947 championship was eighty years old. When she inquired if she might have a younger caddie, she was informed that the youngest they had was seventy-five.

Teeing off in the final, Babe turned and saluted the Union Jack flying from a nearby flagpole, which the crowd loved. Then she noticed a large American flag stretched across the clubhouse roof. She dropped to her knees and bowed three times in its direction—to a roar from the gallery.

So popular was the Babe that virtually every shop in town closed down on the day of the finals. In stores up and down the streets, there were signs posted in the windows: "Closed for day. Gone to see the Babe."

The Babe claimed a seventeen-tournament winning streak and liked to boast that it was one record "no one will ever touch."

Some of her fellow players, however, were skeptical.

"She did win thirteen straight but then things get a little fuzzy," recalls Betty Hicks. "Babe never minded improving on stories about herself."

Babe was playing in the 1950 Western Open when she learned that her mother had died. She tried to arrange for a flight back to Texas but was unsuccessful.

As she sat sobbing in the locker room, a young Betsy Rawls tried to console her.

"What will you do, Babe?" Rawls asked.

"I'm gonna go out and win it for my mother," Babe said. And she did.

Babe Zaharias came to the 1954 U.S. Women's Open at Salem Country Club after undergoing surgery for colon cancer. No one gave her much of a chance of ever playing golf, let alone competitive golf, again. The thought that she might win the LPGA's most prestigious championship was all but out of the question.

But in an almost superhuman display of courage and determination, an exhausted Zaharias not only won but she crushed the field, beating runner-up Betty Hicks by twelve strokes. Later, during the awards ceremony, she broke down.

"When I was sick, I prayed 'Please God, let me win again'— and he did. He answered my prayers," she said.

Two years later, she finally succumbed to the cancer. She was forty-five.

FUZZY ZOELLER

Fuzzy Zoeller, who won both a Masters and a U.S. Open along with eight other tournaments during his PGA Tour career, was a free spirit who is one of the game's most popular players.

For most of his career, he suffered from a bad back. One day a writer asked him how long he planned to keep playing.

"As long as there's enough Advil and vodka to go around," Zoeller joked.

As he approached his fiftieth birthday, he was asked what he thought about the young players on Tour.

"They eat bananas and drink fruit drinks and then go right to bed after dinner," Zoeller said. "What the hell kind of life is that?"

INDEX

Will, George, 113
Wind, Herbert Warren, 75, 161–64
Winged Foot Golf Club, 14, 69, 70, 165
Woods, Earl, 40
Woods, Tiger, 28–29, 30, 40, 107, 139–40, 169, 171–73
Woosnam, Ian, 44–45, 131
World Cup matches, 7

World Golf Hall of Fame, 117

Y
Yancey, Bert, 73
Yates, Charlie, 3, 6, 161
Young, Kathy, 34

Z
Zaharias, Babe, 174–79
Zoeller, Fuzzy, 181